A PHILOSOPHY
OF WALKING

A PHILOSOPHY
OF WALKING

FRÉDÉRIC GROS

Translated by John Howe

VERSO
London • New York

Supported using public funding by
**ARTS COUNCIL
ENGLAND**

This book has been selected to receive financial assistance from English PEN's 'PEN Translates!' programme, supported by Arts Council England. English PEN exists to promote literature and our understanding of it, to uphold writers' freedoms around the world, to campaign against the persecution and imprisonment of writers for stating their views, and to promote the friendly co-operation of writers and the free exchange of ideas. www.englishpen.org

This English-language edition published by Verso 2014
Translation © John Howe 2014
First published as Marcher, une philosophie
© Carnets Nord, 2009

1 3 5 7 9 10 8 6 4 2

Verso
UK: 6 Meard Street, London W1F 0EG
US: 20 Jay Street, Suite 1010, Brooklyn, NY 11201
www.versobooks.com

Verso is the imprint of New Left Books

ISBN-13: 978-1-78168-270-8 (HBK)
ISBN-13: 978-1-78168-629-4 (EXPORT)
eISBN-13: 978-1-78168-271-5 (US)
eISBN-13: 978-1-78168-644-7 (UK)

British Library Cataloguing in Publication Data
A catalogue record for this book is available from the British Library

Library of Congress Cataloging-in-Publication Data

Gros, Frédéric.
[Marcher, une philosophie. English]
A philosophy of walking : / Frédéric Gros ; translated by John Howe.
pages cm
ISBN 978-1-78168-270-8 (alk. paper)
1. Walking--Philosophy. I. Title.
B105.W25G7613 2014
128'.4--dc23

2013045065

Typeset in Trinité by MJ & N Gavan, Truro, Cornwall
Printed and bound by CPI Group (UK) Ltd, Croydon, CR0 4YY

To Daniel Deffert,
who has trusted me.

We do not belong to those who have ideas only among books, when stim-
ulated by books. It is our habit to think outdoors – walking, leaping,
climbing, dancing, preferably on lonely mountains or near the sea where
even the trails become thoughtful.

Friedrich Nietzsche, *The Gay Science*

Contents

CONTENTS

Walking Is Not a Sport

Walking is not a sport.

Sport is a matter of techniques and rules, scores and competition, necessitating lengthy training: knowing the postures, learning the right movements. Then, a long time later, come improvisation and talent.

Sport is keeping score: what's your ranking? Your time? Your place in the results? Always the same division between victor and vanquished that there is in war – there is a kinship between war and sport, one that honours war and dishonours sport: respect for the adversary; hatred of the enemy.

Sport also obviously means cultivation of endurance, of a taste for effort, for discipline. An ethic. A labour.

But then again it is material: reviews, spectacles, a market.

It is performance. Sport gives rise to immense mediatic ceremonies, crowded with consumers of brands and images. Money invades it to empty souls, medical science to construct artificial bodies.

Walking is not a sport. Putting one foot in front of the other is child's play. When walkers meet, there is no result, no time: the walker may say which way he has come, mention the best path for viewing the landscape, what can be seen from this or that promontory.

Efforts have nevertheless been made to create a new market in accessories: revolutionary shoes, incredible socks, high-performance trousers ... the sporting spirit is being surreptitiously introduced, you no longer walk but do a 'trek'. Pointed staffs are on sale to give walkers the appearance of improbable skiers. But none of that goes very far. It can't go far.

Walking is the best way to go more slowly than any other method that has ever been found. To walk, you need to start with two legs. The rest is optional. If you want to go faster, then don't walk, do something else: drive, slide or fly. Don't walk. And when you are walking, there is only one sort of performance that counts: the brilliance of the sky, the splendour of the landscape. Walking is not a sport.

Once on his feet, though, man does not stay where he is.

2

Freedoms

First of all, there is the *suspensive* freedom that comes by walking, even a simple short stroll: throwing off the burden of cares, forgetting business for a time. You choose to leave the office behind, go out, stroll around, think about other things. With a longer excursion of several days, the process of self-liberation is accentuated: you escape the constraints of work, throw off the yoke of routine. But how could walking make you feel this freedom more than a long journey?

Because, after all, other equally tiresome constraints make themselves felt: the weight of the rucksack, the length of the stages, the uncertain weather (threat of rain, of storms, of murderous heat), the primitive accommodation, things like that ... Yet only walking manages to free us from our illusions about the essential.

As such, it is still ruled by powerful necessities. To complete a given stage you have to walk so many hours, meaning so many paces; scope for improvisation is limited, you aren't wandering down garden paths and you have to turn the right way at junctions, or you'll regret it. When fog shrouds the mountains or rain starts to fall in sheets you have to continue, to keep going. Food and water are subject to detailed advance planning, depending on routes and sources. And I am not talking about discomfort, although the real miracle is that one is happy not despite that, but because of it. What I mean is that not having an infinite choice of food or drink, being subject to the inevitability of weather in all its moods, and relying only on one's steady pace – all this quickly makes the profusion of what is available (merchandise, transport, networking), the easy access to facilities (to communicate, to buy, to move about), seem like dependencies. These micro-liberations all constitute accelerations of the system, which imprisons you all the more strongly. But whatever liberates you from time and space *alienates you from speed*.

To someone who has never had the experience, a simple description of the walker's condition quickly appears an absurdity, an aberration, a form of voluntary servitude. Because the city-dweller tends spontaneously to interpret such activity in terms of deprivation, whereas the walker considers it a liberation to be disentangled from the web of exchanges, no longer reduced to a junction in the network redistributing information, images and goods; to see that these things have only the reality and importance you give them. Not only does your world not collapse within these disconnected moments, but those connections suddenly appear to be burdensome, stifling, over-restrictive entanglements.

Freedom then is a mouthful of bread, a draught of cool water, and the open country. That said, rejoicing in that suspensive freedom, happy to set off, one is also happy to return. It's a blessing in parentheses, freedom in an escapade lasting a couple of days or less. Nothing has really changed when you return. And the old inertias are back at once: speed, neglect of the self, of others, excitement and fatigue. The appeal of simplicity has lasted for the time of a hike. 'The fresh air's done you good.' A blink of liberation, and straight back to the grindstone.

The second freedom is more aggressive and rebellious. Walking only permits a temporary 'disconnection' from our daily lives: escape from the web for a few days, a brief out-of-system experience wandering untrodden paths. But one can also decide on a complete break.

The appeal of transgression, the call of the great outdoors are easily found in the writings of Kerouac or Snyder: throwing off moronic conventions, the soporific security of four walls, the boredom of the Same, the wear of repetition, the chilliness of the well-heeled and their hatred of change. The need to provoke departures, transgressions, to give substance at last to folly and dreams. The decision to walk (to head somewhere far off, anywhere, to try something else) can be understood this time as the Call of the Wild.

When walking in this mode we discover the immense vigour of starry night skies, elemental energies, and our appetites follow: they are enormous, and our bodies are satisfied. When you have slammed the world's door, there is nothing left to hold you: pavements no longer guide your steps (the path, a hundred thousand times repeated, of the return to the fold). Crossroads shimmer like hesitant stars, you rediscover the tremulous fear of choosing, a vertiginous freedom.

This time, there's no question of freeing yourself from artifice to taste simple joys. Instead there is the promise of meeting a freedom head-on as an outer limit of the self and of the human, an internal overflowing of a rebellious Nature that goes beyond you. Walking can provoke these excesses: surfeits of fatigue that make the mind wander, abundances of beauty that turn the soul over, excesses of drunkenness on the peaks, the high passes (where the body explodes). Walking ends by awakening this rebellious, archaic part of us: our appetites become rough and uncompromising, our impulses inspired. Because walking puts us on the vertical axis of life: swept along by the torrent that rushes just beneath us.

What I mean is that by walking you are not going to meet yourself. By walking, you escape from the very idea of identity, the temptation to be someone, to have a name and a history. Being someone is all very well for smart parties where everyone is telling their story, it's all very well for psychologists' consulting rooms. But isn't being someone also a social obligation which trails in its wake – for one has to be faithful to the self-portrait – a stupid and burdensome fiction? The freedom in walking lies in not being anyone; for the walking body has no history, it is just an eddy in the stream of immemorial life.

So we are a moving two-legged beast, just a pure force among big trees, just a cry. For often, while walking, we shout to assert our recovered animal presence. No doubt, in the great liberation exalted by the beat generation of Ginsberg and Burroughs, in that debauch of energy that was meant to tear up our lives and blow sky-high the dens of the submissive, walking in the mountains was just one means among others: others that included the drugs, the booze and the orgies through which we hoped to attain innocence.

But a dream can be glimpsed in that freedom: walking to express rejection of a rotten, polluted, alienating, shabby civilization. As Kerouac writes in The Dharma Bums:

i've been reading whitman, you know what he says, cheer up slaves, and horrify foreign despots, he means that's the attitude for the bard, the zen lunacy bard of old desert paths, see the whole thing is a world full of rucksack wanderers, dharma bums refusing to subscribe to the general demand that they consume production and there have to work for the privilege of consuming, all that crap they didn't really want anyway such as refrigerators, tv sets, cars, at least new fancy cars, certain hair oils and deodorants and general junk you finally always see a week later in the garbage anyway, all of them imprisoned in a system of work, produce, consume, work, produce, consume, i see a vision of a great rucksack revolution thousands or even millions of young americans wandering around with rucksacks.

The walker's last freedom is more uncommon. It is a third stage, after the rediscovery of simple joys and the reconquest of the primitive animal: the freedom of *renunciation*. Heinrich Zimmer, one of the great writers on Indian civilizations, tells us that Hindu philosophy distinguishes four stages on the journey through life. The first is that of the pupil, the student, the disciple. Thus in the morning of life, the essential tasks are to obey the master's injunctions, absorb his lessons, submit to criticism and conform to the principles laid down. It is a time for receiving and accepting. In the second stage the man, now adult, in the midday of his life, becomes the master of a house, married, responsible for a family: he manages his property as well as he can, contributes to the upkeep of the priests, exercises a trade or skill, submits to social constraints and imposes them on others. He agrees to wear the social masks that define a role for him in society and in the family.

Later, in the afternoon of his life, when the children are ready to take over, the man can abandon all social duties, family expenses and economic concerns, to become a hermit. This is the stage of 'withdrawal to the forest', in which through contemplation and meditation he familiarizes himself with what has always lain unchanged within us, waiting for us to awaken it: the eternal Self, transcending masks, functions, identities, histories.

And the pilgrim eventually succeeds the hermit, in what should be the endless, glorious summer evening of our lives: a life henceforth dedicated to travel in which endless walking, in one direction and another, illustrates the harmonization of the nameless Self with the omnipresent heart of the World. The sage has now renounced everything and attained the highest level of freedom: that of perfect detachment. He is no longer involved, either in himself or in the world. Indifferent to past and future alike, he is nothing other than the eternal present of coexistence. And as we know from the pilgrimage diaries of Swami Ramdas, it is when we renounce everything that everything is given to us, in abundance. Everything: meaning the intensity of presence itself.

During long cross-country wanders, you do glimpse that freedom of pure renunciation. When you walk for a long time, there comes a moment when you no longer know how many hours have passed, or how many more will be needed to get there; you feel on your shoulders the weight of the bare necessities, you tell yourself that's quite enough – that really nothing more is needed to keep body and soul together – and you feel you could carry on like this for days, for centuries. You can hardly remember where you are going or why; that is as meaningless as your history, or what the time is. And you feel free, because whenever you remember the former signs of your commitments in hell – name, age, profession, CV – it all seems absolutely derisory, minuscule, insubstantial.

3

Why I Am Such a
Good Walker – Nietzsche

Sit as little as possible; do not believe any idea that was not born in the open air and of free movement – in which the muscles do not also revel. All prejudices emanate from the bowels. – Sitting still (I said it once already) – is the real sin against the Holy Ghost.

Friedrich Nietzsche, *Ecce Homo*

R uptures, Nietzsche wrote, are difficult, because of the suffering caused by the removal of a bond. But in its place, we soon receive a boost. Nietzsche's life was to be made up of these detachments, these breaks, these isolations: from the world, society, travelling companions, colleagues, wives, friends, relations. But every deepening of his solitude signified a further extension of his freedom: no

11

explanations to give, no compromises to stand in his way, his vision clear and detached.

Nietzsche was a remarkable walker, tireless. He mentioned it all the time. Walking out of doors was as it were the *natural element* of his oeuvre, the invariable accompaniment to his writing.

His life can be divided into four main acts, the first covering his formative years, from his birth in 1844 to his appointment as professor of philology at the University of Basle. His father was a pastor, a good and upright man who died young, when Friedrich was four years old. The young Nietzsche liked to imagine himself the last scion of a noble Polish lineage (the Nietzskis).

After his father's death he became the pampered darling of his mother, grandmother and sister, the object of intense solicitude. Highly intelligent, the boy received a classical education at the renowned (and tough) Pforta secondary school. There he was subjected to an iron regime whose efficacy he was to recognize later in life, based on the Greek equation: you must know how to obey in order to know how to command. His loving and admiring mother hoped that he would use his brilliant intellect in God's service, seeing him as a theologian. He was a vigorous boy with excellent health, afflicted only by severe short-sightedness, doubtless very badly corrected.

A brilliant academic career in philology followed at the University of Bonn, then at Leipzig. At the precocious age of twenty-four, he was appointed professor of philology at the University of Basle, on the recommendation of the philologist and librarian Friedrich Ritschi. The second act opened.

For ten years he taught Greek philology, ten years of struggle and difficulty. The workload was enormous: in addition to his lectures at the university, he was required to lecture at the town's main secondary school (the Pedagogium). But Nietzsche's interests extended beyond philology alone. Attracted by music at an early age, he was later fascinated by philosophy; but it was the science of philology that had welcomed him. And he embraced it in return, slightly unhappily, for it was not his true vocation. It did enable him at least to read the Greek authors: tragedians (Aeschylus, Sophocles), poets (Homer, Hesiod), philosophers (Heraclitus, Anaximander) and historians (especially Diogenes Laertius, because, he said, his writings portrayed men, over and above systems). The first year went very well: he worked with fervour on his lectures, enjoyed success among the students, found new colleagues – one of whom, Franz Overbeck, professor of theology, became his dear and faithful friend. The friend through thick and thin, the one who is called on to help; the one who went to look for him in Turin after the catastrophe.

It was in 1869 that Nietzsche made a trip to Lucerne, going on to Tribschen where he made his emotional visit to the 'Master' (Wagner) in the latter's immense, monumental house. There he was much taken with Cosima (whom he would call, in the letters he wrote after going mad, his 'Princess Ariane, my beloved – a prejudice makes

me a man, but it is true that I have long frequented them' –
January 1889).

The enthusiasm, academic ardour and bounding health
did not last long, however. Fainting fits and seizures started
to occur. The body was avenging a series of bad mistakes.

Professional trouble began with the appearance in 1871
of The Birth of Tragedy, which rendered professional phi-
lologists speechless, often with rage. Could he really have
meant to write such a work? Less the outcome of serious
research than of vague, metaphysical intuitions: the eternal
conflict between chaos and form. He was troubled in his
friendships, too. He went regularly to Bayreuth to attend
the Master's annual consecration, returned to Tribschen,
became a travelling companion in Europe, but came more
and more to understand that Wagner's fanatical dogmatism
and arrogance represented all that he most execrated, and
that above all the music made him ill.

Wagner's music, he was to write, drowns you, it's a mar-
asmus, you have to 'swim' continuously in it, it submerges
you in a throbbing, chaotic wave. You lose your footing
when you listen to it. Rossini on the other hand makes you
want to dance. Not to mention Bizet's Carmen. Misfortune
in love plagued him too: refusal after refusal answered
his – somewhat abrupt – proposals of marriage. And lastly,
social failure, for he did not manage to take root either in
the worldly clamour of Bayreuth or in academic and intellectual circles.

Everything became more difficult. Every term was harder,
more impossible. Increasingly he was seized by terrible

headaches that kept him in bed, lying in the dark, gasping with agony. His eyes hurt, he could hardly read or write. Each quarter-hour of reading or writing cost him hours of migraine. He asked to be read to, for his eyes wavered on contact with the page.

Nietzsche tried to compromise, asking to be discharged from one course, and soon after even from his teaching obligations at the secondary school. He obtained a year off to breathe, recover, gather his strength. But nothing worked.

Nevertheless, what he meant at the time to be a restorative carried the mark of his future destiny: long walks and great solitude, two remedies against throbbing, terrible pain. Flight from the arousal, the demands, the agitations of the world, always paid for in hours of suffering. And walking, walking for hours at a time to disperse, divert, forget the hammering in his temples. He had not yet become fascinated by the hard minerality of high mountains or the scented aridity of the South's rocky paths. He walked mainly beside lakes (Lake Léman, with Carl von Gersdorff, six hours a day), or plunged into the shade of forests (pine forests, at Steinabad near the southern end of the Black Forest: 'I am walking a lot, through the forest, and having tremendous conversations with myself').

By August 1877 he was at Rosenlaui, living as a hermit: 'If only I could have a little house somewhere like this; I would walk for six or eight hours a day, composing thoughts that I would later jot down on paper.'

But nothing really helped. The pain was too fierce. Migraine attacks kept him in bed for days at a time, painful vomiting kept him awake all night. His eyes hurt, and his sight started to fade. In May 1879 he submitted his resignation to the university.

~

Now began the third major period of his life: ten years between the summer of 1879 and the beginning of 1889. He was living on the combination of three small grants that enabled him to live very modestly, stay in small inns, afford the train fare from the mountains to the sea, from the sea to the mountains, or sometimes to Venice to visit Peter Gast. It was at this time that he became the peerless walker of legend. Nietzsche walked, he walked as others work. And he worked while he was walking.

The first summer he discovered his mountain, the Upper Engadine, and the following year his village, Sils-Maria. The air was clear there, the wind brisk, the light piercing. He detested stifling heat, so spent every summer there until the collapse (apart from the year of Lou). He wrote to his friends Overbeck and Köselitz that he had found his own nature, his element; and to his mother he wrote that he had found 'the best paths that the half-blind man I have become could hope for, and the most tonic air' (July 1879). This was his landscape, and he felt related to it 'by blood, nay even more to me'. Starting that first summer, he walked, alone, for up to eight hours a day, and wrote The Wanderer and His Shadow. All of it except a few lines was thought out en route, and scribbled down in pencil in six small notebooks.

He spent the winter in southern towns, essentially Genoa, the bay of Rapallo and later Nice ('I walk on average an hour in the morning, three hours in the afternoon, at a good pace – always the same route: it is beautiful enough to bear repetition', March 1888), Menton just once ('I have found eight walks', November 1884). The hills were his writing bench, the sea his great arch ('The sea and the pure sky! Why did I so torture myself in the past?' January 1881).

Thus walking, looking down on the world and men, he composed in the open air, imagined, discovered, grew excited, was frightened by what he found, astonished and gripped by what came to him on his walks:

> The intensity of my feelings makes me laugh and shiver at the same time – it has happened several times that I have been unable to leave my room for the ridiculous reason that my eyes were red – and for what cause? Just that on the previous day during my long walks I had wept too much, and not sentimental tears but tears of happiness, singing and staggering, taken over by a new gaze that marks my privilege over the men of today.

In those ten years he wrote his greatest books, from *The Dawn* to *On the Genealogy of Morality*, from *The Gay Science* to *Beyond Good and Evil*, not forgetting *Zarathustra*. He became the hermit ('find myself once again a hermit, and do ten hours a day of hermit's walking', July 1880); the solitary, the wanderer.

~

Walking here is not, as with Kant, a distraction from work, a minimal ablution enabling the body to recover from sitting in one place, stooping, bent double. For Nietzsche, it was the work's precondition. More than a relaxation, or even an accompaniment, walking was truly his element.

> We do not belong to those who have ideas only among books, when stimulated by books. It is our habit to think outdoors – walking, leaping, climbing, dancing, preferably on lonely mountains or near the sea where even the trails become thoughtful. Our first questions about the value of a book, of a human being, or a musical composition are: Can they walk? Even more, can they dance?

Many others have written their books solely from their reading of other books, so that many books exude the stuffy odour of libraries. By what does one judge a book? By its smell (and even more, as we shall see, by its cadence). Its smell: far too many books have the fusty odour of reading rooms or desks. Lightless rooms, poorly ventilated. The air circulates badly between the shelves and becomes saturated with the scent of mildew, the slow decomposition of paper, ink undergoing chemical change. The air is loaded with miasmas there. Other books breathe a livelier air; the bracing air of outdoors, the wind of high mountains, even the icy gust of the high crags buffeting the body; or in the morning, the cool scented air of southern paths through the pines. These books breathe. They are not overloaded, saturated, with dead, vain erudition.

How quickly we guess how someone has come by his ideas; whether it was while sitting in front of his inkwell, with a pinched belly, his head bowed low over the paper – in which case we are quickly finished with his book, too! Cramped intestines betray themselves – you can bet on that – no less than closet air, closet ceilings, closet narrowness.

There is also the quest for a different light. Libraries are always too dark. The heaping, the piling up, the infinite juxtaposition of volumes, the height of the stacks, everything converges to obstruct daylight.

Other books reflect piercing mountain light, or the sea sparkling in sunshine. And above all, colours. Libraries are grey, and grey are the books written in them: overloaded with quotations, references, footnotes, explicatory prudence, indefinite refutations.

Think of the scribe's body: his hands, his feet, his shoulders and legs. Think of the book as an expression of physiology. In all too many books the reader can sense the seated body, doubled up, stooped, shrivelled in on itself. The walking body is unfolded and tensed like a bow: opened to wide spaces like a flower to the sun, exposed torso, tensed legs, lean arms.

Our first question about the value of a book, of a human being, or a musical composition are: can they walk?

Books by authors imprisoned in their studies, grafted to their chairs, are heavy and indigestible. They are born of a compilation of the other books on the table. They are like fattened geese: crammed with citations, stuffed with references, weighed down with annotations. They are weighty, obese, *boring*, and are read slowly, with difficulty. Books made from other books, by comparing lines with other lines, by repeating what others have said of what still others have thoroughly explained. They verify, specify, rectify; a phrase becomes a paragraph, a whole chapter. A book becomes the commentary of a hundred books on a single sentence from another book.

An author who composes while walking, on the other hand, is free from such bonds; his thought is not the slave of other volumes, not swollen with verifications, nor weighted with the thought of others. It contains no explanation owed to anyone: just thought, judgement, decision. It is thought born of a movement, an impulse. In it we can feel the body's elasticity, the rhythm of a dance. It retains and expresses the energy, the springiness of the body. Here is thought about the thing itself, without the scrambling, the fogginess, the barriers, the customs clearances of culture and tradition. The result will not be long and meticulous exegesis, but thoughts that are light and profound. That is really the challenge: the lighter a thought, the more it rises, and becomes profound by rising – vertiginously – above the thick marshes of conviction, opinion, established thought. While books conceived in the library are on the contrary superficial and heavy. They remain on the level of recopying.

Think while walking, walk while thinking, and let writing be but the light pause, as the body on a walk rests in contemplation of wide open spaces.

This leads neatly, in conclusion, to Nietzsche's eulogy of the foot: we write only with the hand; we write well 'only with our feet'. The foot is an excellent witness, perhaps the most reliable. We should notice if, while reading, the foot 'pricks up its ears' – for the foot listens. We read in Zarathustra's second 'dance song': 'My toes rose up to listen; for a dancer's ears are carried on his toes' – when it shivers with pleasure because invited to dance, at the beginning, *outside*.

To judge the quality of a piece of music, we should trust the foot. If, when listening, the wish arises in the foot to mark the rhythm, it's a good sign. All music is an invitation to lightness. Wagner's music depresses the foot in this respect: it makes it panic, it forgets how to place itself. Worse still, it languishes, drags, turns this way and that, gets irritated. While listening to Wagner, as Nietzsche tells us in his last texts, it's impossible to feel the desire to dance, for one is submerged in swirling meanders of music, vague torrents, muddled yearnings.

> I can no longer breathe with ease when this music begins to have its effect upon me ... my foot immediately begins to feel indignant at it and rebels: for what it needs is time, dance, march; even the young German Kaiser could not march to Wagner's Imperial March; what my foot demands in the first place from music is that ecstasy which lies in good walking, stepping and dancing.

Nietzsche walked all day long, scribbling down here and there what the walking body – confronting sky, sea, glaciers – breathed into his thought. I am, says Zarathustra, 'a wanderer and mountain-climber, said he to his heart, I love not the plains, and it seemeth I cannot long sit still.

And whatever may still overtake me as fate and experience – a wandering will be therein, and a mountain-climbing: in the end one experienceth only oneself.'

With Nietzsche, walking meant rising, scrambling, climbing. At Sorrento in 1876, he chose for his daily walks the mountain paths behind the town. From Nice, he liked to climb the path leading straight uphill to the small village of Èze, where he was almost vertically above the sea. From Sils-Maria he took the paths climbing towards high valleys. At Rapallo, he conquered Monte Allegro ('the principal summit in the region').

In Gérard de Nerval's case, forest paths – flat labyrinths – and gentle plains invite the walker's body to softness, to languor. And memories arise like eddying mists. The air is more bracing with Nietzsche, and above all sharp, transparent. The thought is trenchant, the body wide awake, trembling. So instead of sluggishly returning memories there are judgements being made: diagnoses, discoveries, interpolations, verdicts.

The climbing body demands effort; it is under continuous tension. It is an aid to thought in the pursuit of examination: pushing on a little further, a little higher. It's important not to weaken, but to mobilize energy to advance, to place the foot firmly and hoist the body slowly, then restore balance. So with thought: an idea to rise to something even more astonishing, unheard-of, *new*. And then again: it is a matter of gaining altitude. There are thoughts that can only occur at 6,000 feet above the plains and mournful shores.

'Six thousand feet beyond man and time.' That day I happened
to be wandering through the woods alongside of the Lake of
Silvaplana, and I halted not far from Surlei, beside a huge rock
that towered aloft like a pyramid. It was then that the thought
struck me.

To know that the world swarms under his feet. *Suave turba
magna* ... how sweet it is to perceive, through the clear glacial
air, the motionless crowd stagnating on the spot far below?
But no, Nietzsche's aristocratic outlook does not extend to
such arrogant contempt.

Rather it is that for thinking one needs a detached
outlook, to be at a distance, to have clear air. One needs to
be unconstrained to think far. And what then do details,
definitions, exactitudes mean? It is the armature of human
destiny that one needs to see laid out. From very high up
one sees the movement of landscapes, the design of hills.
And thus with history: Antiquity, Christianity, modernity ...
what do they produce in the way of archetypes, characters, essences? The moment your nose is buried in dates, in
facts, everything falls back on your own clenched peculiarity. Whereas the need is to construct fictions, myths, *general*
destinies.

We still need to climb a good stretch of road, slowly, but
ever higher, in order to reach a properly detached point of
view on our old civilization.

Something clear, like the line of a road. Not the sedentary
man's stupid failure to understand, but rather the compassion Nietzsche had always recognized as his problem ('ever
since I was a child, I have never ceased to notice that "pity

is my greatest peril"', September 1884). That compassion on seeing human beings busying themselves, going to Mass or entertainments, seeking recognition from their peers, becoming mired in sad images: poor in themselves. While from above, from a detached position, one understands what made mankind sick: the poison of sedentary moralities.

Then too, during very long walks, there is always that emergence through a high pass where another landscape appears all of a sudden. After the effort, the long climb, the body turns round and sees at its feet the offered immensity; or, at a turn in the path, it witnesses a transformation: a range of mountains, a splendour lying in wait. Many aphorisms are built on these reversals of perspective, these final exclamations where something else is unveiled, the secret of a discovery like a new landscape, and the jubilation that accompanies it.

Finally it is worth mentioning what Eternal Recurrence owes to the experience of walking (bearing in mind, too, that Nietzsche's long excursions were made on known paths, signposted routes that he liked to repeat). When one has walked a long way to reach the turning in the path that discloses an anticipated view, and that view appears, there is always a vibration of the landscape. It is repeated in the walker's body. The harmony of the two presences, like two strings in tune, each feeding off the vibration of the other, is like an endless relaunch. Eternal Recurrence is the unfolding in a continuous circle of the repetition of those two affirmations, the circular transformation of the vibration of the presences. The walker's immobility facing that of the landscape ... it is the very intensity of that co-presence that gives birth to an indefinite circularity of exchanges: I have always been here, tomorrow, contemplating this landscape.

~

By the middle of the 1880s, however, Nietzsche was complaining that he couldn't walk as well as he should. He was suffering from back pain and had to spend long periods reclining in a chair. He persisted nevertheless, but his walks became shorter. Sometimes he even took companions along. The 'hermit of Sils', as he was called, began often to walk in the company of protectresses, young female admirers: Helen Zimmern who had translated his text on Schopenhauer, Meta von Salis, a young aristocrat who brought him the heavyweight endorsement of the local nobility, the student Resa von Schirnhofer, and Hélène Druscowitz, newly awakened to philosophy.

These less solitary walks were no longer the same. Nietzsche increasingly played the urbane gent, the gallant surrounded by cultivated women. He took them to see the rock where he had received illumination on Eternal Recurrence, confided poignantly on his friendship with Wagner. And pain slowly took hold of him once more: from 1886 he was complaining of horribly prolonged migraine attacks. The vomiting reappeared too. After each excursion he needed several days to recover. Sometimes a long walk left him exhausted for days.

Towns increasingly disgusted him: he found them dirty and expensive. During his winter sojourns in Nice, he could not afford to pay for south-facing rooms, and suffered from the cold. At Sils, in summer, the weather often seemed bad to him. Venice he found atrociously depressing. His condition worsened.

There was one last metamorphosis. The final act of his life opened like a song of renewal, an ode to joy: he discovered Turin for the first time in April 1888. It was like a revelation: the city was absolutely classical 'for the feet as for the eyes – and what cobblestones!' Long walks on the banks of the Po enchanted him. After a final summer at Sils, grimmer than ever, he returned to Turin in September. The same miracle, a renewal of joy.

There was a sudden access of happiness, and of magnificent health. The ailments all went away as if by magic, and he now felt his body only as a lightness, a bounding momentum. He was working quickly and well. His eyes no longer hurt; his stomach could digest anything. In a few months he dashed off several books, like a powder-train. He walked with passionate dedication, in the evening accumulating notes for his planned four works on the 'transvaluation of values'.

But early in 1889, Jacob Burckhardt received a letter from Nietzsche dated 6 January. It worried him: it was the letter of one demented, a madman ('In the final analysis, I would rather have been a professor at Basle than God; but I hesitated to take egotism to the point of dispensing with the creation of the world'). Other letters sent in that first week of January reveal the same state. Nietzsche signed himself Dionysus, or the Crucified ('once discovered, it was easy for you to find me; the difficulty henceforth will be to lose me').

Burckhardt immediately informed Overbeck, who hurried to Turin, where he struggled to find Nietzsche in his small lodging in Davide Fino's house. His landlords were at a loss: Nietzsche had become uncontrollable. He had clung, weeping, to the neck of a horse whose driver had whipped the animal. He had wandered around mumbling incoherent ideas, harangued passers-by, and gate-crashed funerals, claiming to be the deceased. Overbeck found Nietzsche slumped in an armchair, haggard, looking in dismay at the proofs of his latest book. He looked up and, seeing his old friend, sprang up in surprise and embraced him: he had recognized him. And he wept, held on and wept; as if, Overbeck wrote, he could see the abyss opening beneath him. Then he sat down and curled up once more.

Nietzsche had become extremely grand: apparently he was a prince and was owed every courtesy. He was coaxed, bawling songs and shouting, to the station and into a train. He was mad. His friends managed to get him as far as Basle by saying that His Excellency was awaited there for a reception worthy of him.

He was admitted to the clinic in Basle, then was sent from there to Jena, without noticeable improvement. Eventually his mother took him in, at Naumburg. She cared for him until her own death with love, patience and devotion. She washed and tidied him, consoled him, took him for walks, watched over him night and day. For seven years.

Nietzsche increasingly walled himself up in silence, or made incoherent speeches. His sentences were shreds, vestiges; he no longer thought. Sometimes, still, he improvised for a while on the piano. He no longer had migraines, or eye trouble.

His mother understood that only long walks did him any good. But it wasn't easy: he would take against passers-by in the street, utter meaningless bellows. She soon shortened their outings, because she was ashamed, ashamed of her big forty-four-year-old son who roared like a bear, or cursed into the wind. Sometimes she would take him out in the late afternoon, when people were indoors and he could yell without upsetting anyone.

Soon, however, the body itself became obstructive: paralysis crept gradually through his spine. He was back in a wheelchair in which people pushed him around, took him out. He stared at his hands for hours at a time, first one, then the other, or held books upside down, mumbling. He lay helpless in a chair, while others bustled around him. He had regressed to childhood. His mother wheeled him up and down the verandah. After autumn 1894 he could only recognize his immediate family, his mother and sister, and remained prostrate, usually motionless, staring at his hands. Very rarely he would say something: 'When all is said and done, death'; 'I don't sow horses'; 'More light'.

The decline was slow, ineluctable. His eyes sank into his skull, their gaze vertiginously withdrawn. He died on 25 August 1900, in Weimar.

It is probable that I will be, for men still to come, an inevitability, the inevitable – it is therefore entirely possible that one day I will fall silent, for love of humanity!!!

4

Outside

Walking means being out of doors, outside, 'in the fresh air', as they say. Walking causes the inversion of town-dweller's logics, and even of our most widespread condition.

When you go 'outside' it is always to pass from one 'inside' to another: from house to office, from your place to the nearest shops. You go out to do something, somewhere else. Outside is a transition: the thing that separates; almost an obstacle between here and there. But one that has no value of its own. You make it from your place to the tube station in all weathers, with a hurried body, a mind still half-occupied with domestic details but already projected towards work obligations, legs galloping while the hand nervously checks the pockets to ensure nothing has been forgotten. Outside hardly exists: it is like a big separating corridor, a tunnel, an immense airlock.

It's true that you can go out sometimes just to 'get some air'; some relief from the weighty immobility of objects and walls. Because you feel stifled indoors, you take a breather while the sun is shining out there; it just seems unfair to deny yourself the exposure to light. Then, yes, you go out and take a step round the block, simply to be outside rather than to go here or there. To feel the lively freshness of a spring breeze, or the fragile warmth of winter sunshine. An interlude, a managed pause. Children, too, go out just for the sake of it. 'Going out' at that age means playing, running, laughing. Later it will mean seeing their friends, escaping from parents, doing something different. But more often than not, once again outside is placed between two insides: a stage, a transition. It is some space that takes some time.

Outside. Out of doors. In walks that extend over several days, during major expeditions, everything is inverted. 'Outside' is no longer a transition, but the element in which stability exists. It's the other way round: you go from lodging to lodging, shelter to shelter, and the thing that changes is the infinitely variable 'indoors'. You never sleep twice in the same bed, different hosts put you up each night. Every new décor, every change in ambiance, is a new surprise; the variety of walls, of stones. You stop: the body is tired, night is falling, you need rest. But these interiors are milestones every time, means to help keep you outside for longer: transitions.

Another thing worth mentioning is the strange impression made by your first steps, in the morning. You have looked at the map, chosen your route, said your goodbyes, packed your rucksack, identified the right path, checked its direction. It seems like a kind of hesitation, trampling about slightly, back and forth, as it were punctuations: stopping, checking the direction, turning around on the spot. Then the path opens, you head off, pick up the rhythm. You lift your head, you're on your way, but really just to be walking, to be out of doors. That's it, that's all, and you're there. Outdoors is our element: the exact sensation of living there. You leave one lodging for another, but continuity, what lasts and persists, comes from the surrounding landscapes, the chains of hills that are always there. And it is I who wind through them, I stroll there as if at home: by walking, I take the measure of my dwelling. The obligatory passages, which you traverse and leave behind, are bedrooms for one night, dining rooms for one dinner and one breakfast, the people who run them, the ghosts that inhabit them; but not the landscape.

That is how the big separation between outside and inside is turned upside down by walking. We shouldn't say that we cross mountains and plains, and that we stop at lodgings. It is almost the opposite: for several days I live in a landscape, I slowly take possession of it, I make it my site.

Then that strange morning impression can arise, when you have left the walls of rest behind you, and find yourself with the wind on your face, right in the middle of the world: this is really my home all day long, this is where I am going to dwell by walking.

5

Slowness

I will always remember what he said. We were climbing a steep path in the Italian Alps. Mateo was my senior by at least half a century, being over seventy-five years old at that time. He was whipcord-thin, with big rough hands, a lined face and an erect posture. He kept his arms folded when walking, as if feeling cold, and wore beige canvas trousers.

It was he who taught me to walk. Although I was saying just now: you don't learn to walk, at least here, no technique, no panic about getting it right or not, about doing it this way rather than that, no pressure to pull yourself together, practise, concentrate. Everyone knows how to walk. One foot in front of the other, that's the proper rhythm, the good distance to go somewhere, anywhere. And all you have to do is resume: one foot in front of the other.

I say he 'taught' me for the sake of brevity and effect. We had been walking for several minutes on a climbing path and began to feel a sort of pressure from behind. A group of young people, boisterous, wanting to hurry and overtake us, trod a little noisily to make their presence felt. So we stood aside and let the loud, hurrying troupe pass, and were thanked with slightly smug smiles. It was then, as he watched them recede, that Mateo said: 'Well look, they're afraid they won't get there, wanting to walk at that speed!'

The lesson was that in walking, the authentic sign of assurance is a good slowness. What I mean is a sort of slowness that isn't exactly the opposite of speed. In the first place it's the extreme regularity of paces, a uniformity. Here one might almost say that a good walker glides, or perhaps that his legs rotate, describing circles. A bad walker may sometimes go fast, accelerate, then slow down. His movements are jerky, his legs form clumsy angles. His speed will be made of sudden accelerations, followed by heavy breathing. Large voluntary movements, a new decision every time the body is pushed or pulled, a red perspiring face. Slowness really is the opposite of *haste*. When we reached the summit and caught up with the 'sportsmen', they were sitting down, discussing their time with enthusiasm and making incomprehensible calculations. The reason they were hurrying like that was that they wanted to make a particular time. We stopped for a minute to look at the view. Then, while the group continued to make long commentaries and interminable comparisons, we slowly started back.

The illusion of speed is the belief that it saves time. It looks simple at first sight: finish something in two hours instead of three, gain an hour. It's an abstract calculation, though, done as if each hour of the day were like an hour on the clock, absolutely equal.

But haste and speed accelerate time, which passes more quickly, and two hours of hurry shorten a day. Every minute is torn apart by being segmented, stuffed to bursting. You can pile a mountain of things into an hour. Days of slow walking are very long: they make you live longer, because you have allowed every hour, every minute, every second to breathe, to deepen, instead of filling them up by straining the joints. Hurrying means doing several things at once, and quickly: this; then that; and then something else. When you hurry, time is filled to bursting, like a badly-arranged drawer in which you have stuffed different things without any attempt at order.

Slowness means cleaving perfectly to time, so closely that the seconds fall one by one, drop by drop like the steady dripping of a tap on stone. This stretching of time deepens space. It is one of the secrets of walking: a slow approach to landscapes that gradually renders them familiar. Like the regular encounters that deepen friendship. Thus a mountain skyline that stays with you all day, which you observe in different lights, defines and articulates itself. When you are walking, nothing moves: only imperceptibly do the hills draw closer, the surroundings change. In a train or car, we see a mountain coming towards us. The eye is quick, active, it thinks it has understood everything, grasped it all. When you are walking, nothing really moves: it is rather that presence is slowly established in the body. When we are walking, it isn't so much that we are drawing nearer, more that the things out there become more and more insistent in our body. The landscape is a set of tastes, colours, scents which the body absorbs.

6

The Passion for
Escape – Rimbaud

*I can't give you an address to reply to this, for I don't know personally where
I may find myself dragged next, or by what routes, on the way to where, or
why, or how!*

Arthur Rimbaud, Letter from Aden, 5 May 1884

Verlaine called him 'the man with soles of wind'.
The man himself, when still very young, had
described himself thus: 'I'm a pedestrian, nothing
more.' Rimbaud walked throughout his life.

Obstinately, with passion. Between the ages of fifteen
and seventeen, he walked to reach great cities: the Paris of
literary hopes, to become known in Parnassian circles, to
meet poets like himself, desperately lonely and longing to

be loved (read his poems). To Brussels, to pursue a career in journalism. Between twenty and twenty-four, he several times tried the route to the South, returning home for the winter. Preparation for travel ... There were incessant shuttles between Mediterranean ports (Marseille or Genoa) and Charleville; walking towards the sun. And from the age of twenty-five until his death, desert roads.

~

At fifteen, drawn to the city of poets, and feeling lonely and decidedly redundant in Charleville, Rimbaud took off for Paris, his head full of naïve dreams. He left on foot very early one August morning, without a word to anyone. He walked probably to Givet, and there took the train. But selling his books – valuable ones, for he had been an excellent pupil – did not produce enough money to pay for the full journey to the capital. On arrival at the Gare de Strasbourg, he found the police waiting: he was arrested for theft, deemed a vagabond, and taken immediately to the local police station, then to the Mazas prison. His teacher of rhetoric, the famous Georges Izambard, rushed to his rescue and secured his pupil's release by paying the railway company the unpaid portion of his fare. The line to Charleville being still cut because of the Franco-Prussian war, Rimbaud went to stay at Douai, with his protector's family. There followed a sequence of happy days, talking literature and being spoiled by big sisters. But his mother sent for him.

Barely a month later, Rimbaud sold some more books

and ran away again. He took the train as far as Fumay, then continued on foot, from village to village (Vireux, Givet) along the Meuse. To Charleroi. 'Eight days earlier, I had ripped my ankle-boots on the stones of the roads. I was entering Charleroi.'

There he offered his services to the *Journal de Charleroi*, which turned him down. Rimbaud went on to Brussels, penniless, still on foot, to find, or so he hoped, his protector Izambard. 'I set off, my fists in my torn pockets; my overcoat too was becoming ideal; I was going under the sky, Muse! And I was your vassal; Oh good heavens, what splendid amours I dreamed!'

Fifty kilometres of joyous exclamation, hands in pockets and dreaming of literary glory and love. But Izambard wasn't there. Durand, the teacher's friend, gave him enough to set him on his way. Rimbaud did not go straight home, but to Douai, to his new family: 'It's me, I've come back.' He arrived charged with a poetry born all along the roads – illuminations of flights and escapades – composed to the rhythms of paths and swinging arms.

A poetry of well-being, of festive relaxation in country inns. Satisfaction with the day's progress, the body filled with space. Youth.

'Blissfully happy, I stretched my legs under the table.'

Days and days of walking through golden autumn colours. Laughing outdoor nights, on roadside verges, under the glittering roof of stars.

'My inn was at the sign of the Great Bear. – My stars in the sky making a gentle fuss.'

41

Rimbaud made careful fair copies of his inventions on big white sheets. Happy in the affection of his new family. He was sixteen. On 1 November Rimbaud's mother ('mouth of shadow') ordered Izambard to return her son forthwith, via the police 'to avoid expense'.

In February 1871, with the Franco-Prussian war under way, Rimbaud still dreamed of Paris, of which he had only seen the inside of a prison the first time. Charleville was still in the grip of winter. Arthur took on airs, allowed his hair to grow to an unseemly length, walked proudly up and down the main street smoking a pipe. He fretted and fumed; again without saying anything, secretly, he prepared his next escape. This time he had sold a silver watch, and had enough to pay for a rail ticket to his destination.

By 25 February he was wandering through Paris, gazing excitedly into bookshop windows, wondering what was new in poetry, sleeping in coal barges, living on gathered scraps and leavings, seeking feverishly to make contact with the literary Brotherhood. But it was not a time for literature: the Prussians were coming, the town had veiled itself in darkness. Stomach and pockets empty, Rimbaud crossed the enemy lines to return home, on foot all the way but sometimes given lifts on farm carts. He reached home 'at night, almost naked and suffering from bad bronchitis'.

Did he leave again that spring? Legend or reality? An enigma, anyway ... Will we ever know for sure? Rimbaud would have trembled eagerly at news of the Paris Commune. He must have chafed in Charleville, knowing that they were in rebellion down there, he the author of a communist constitution ... His childhood had been pious, but he had become fiercely republican, rabidly anti-clerical. News of the uprising, in the name of liberty and fraternity, entranced him: 'order is vanquished'. The decree establishing the Commune was issued in March. He is said to have been spotted in Paris in April. But not for certain. Ernest Delahaye recounts that Arthur joined the communard militia, that he enrolled as a sniper at Babylon barracks ... the episode may have lasted a fortnight. Having arrived on a coal barge, he is thought to have returned home on foot, destitute and starving. It's difficult when you have no money.

He returned to Paris for a fourth visit (or was it only the third?). This time, though, was to be the real consecration. Autumn 1871, just as he turned seventeen. This time, too, his mother had been informed: an official trip, almost. Because he was expected there; invited, it would seem, by a smitten Verlaine to whom he had sent his poems ('Come, come quickly, *great dear soul*'). A collection had been organized to pay his train fare. He was carrying his *Bateau ivre* by way of offering, qualification and evidence.

There followed, as we know, three years during which Verlaine kept Rimbaud, three long years of stormy, passionate relations: thoughtless follies, three tormented visits to London together, sordid binges, monstrous storms and sublime reconciliations, until the unhappy pistol shot in Brussels (wounding Rimbaud in the arm) which ended everything. Verlaine went to prison, while his provocateur-victim made several more returns to the starting line

(Charleville or Roche). As always, Rimbaud was bored rigid, but his cavortings with Verlaine had led to his exclusion from literary circles. From his first appearance in Paris his reputation had been that of a filthy brat: a dirty, unpleasant hooligan and inveterate drunkard.

He was twenty in 1875, and had written his *Season in Hell* and *Illuminations*, also (perhaps) a *Spiritual Hunt* which is permanently lost. The publication of *A Season in Hell* had been a sad disaster. He couldn't pay the publisher, and had received only a handful of copies. He was never to see his *Illuminations* in print. A street urchin had transformed the whole of literature in the space of five years. He would never write another poem.

Plenty of letters of course, written in telegraphic style (newsflashes), but not a single poem. He still walked a lot, obstinately. But now he wanted to travel far; alone in his room, he learned languages. He learned German, applied himself to Italian, glanced at Spanish, worked on a Greek-Russian dictionary, doubtless also picked up rudiments of Arabic. For five years, he spent his winters learning. Long walks were for springtime.

In Stuttgart in 1875, he decided to go to Italy. He crossed Switzerland, at first by train, but soon ran short of money and continued on foot, climbing the Saint Gotthard pass, and arrived exhausted in Milan, where a mysterious woman nursed him. He set off to walk to Brindisi, but was laid low by sunstroke on the road between Leghorn and Siena. Repatriated to Marseille, he reached Paris, then Charleville once again.

1876 was a year of adventures, rather than walks. He left for Russia (first having his head shaved), but only got as far as Vienna where he was found half dead and without papers after a beating from a coachman. He enlisted in the Dutch army, but deserted in Salatiga (Dutch East Indies, now Indonesia).

In 1877 he left for Bremen, hoping to reach the Americas, but ended up in Stockholm as the ticket collector on a circus turnstile. He returned to Charleville, and in 1878 boarded a ship to Egypt at Marseille, but quickly fell ill and was repatriated. Returning home on foot, he left for Switzerland. Over the Saint Gotthard again, on foot, to Genoa where he embarked for Cyprus (where he was to become a foreman). But in the spring of 1879 his fever returned and worsened. He went home again. With the first winter chills, however, he headed back to Marseille, but was again stopped by fever, and turned around. It was always the same movement, the same slow oscillation: winter getting bored at home, champing at the bit, learning languages from dictionaries; the rest of the time trying his luck.

In 1880 he left once more, again for Cyprus. From there, after a hurried departure – had he inflicted a mortal wound on a worker? – he pushed southwards for the first time instead of returning to the North: down the Red Sea to Aden. There began the last act of his life, a decade spent mainly between Aden and Harar.

Aden was an oven, with temperatures in the region of 40° Celsius. Rimbaud worked as a supervisor in the selection and sorting of coffee, and was valued by his employers.

An established trader, Alfred Bardey, asked him to open a new agency at Harar in Abyssinia, amid high farming land. At 6,000 feet the climate is temperate. Rimbaud agreed and prepared a caravan. To reach Harar he had to travel some 300 kilometres through jungle, stony deserts and finally forests and mountains, with steep passes. Rimbaud was sometimes mounted but usually had to walk. The caravan advanced slowly. The journey took two weeks.

The boss of the new agency traded, became acclimatized, got bored, became distracted, and organized expeditions. A year in Harar, then back to Aden; then Harar again, and Aden once more. Back and forth on the same gruelling route. He changed jobs as the agency's fortunes fluctuated. Nothing really worked out. He launched mad projects which failed, either soon or straight away. He wanted to amass some money, a bit of capital to set him up for good and bring some peace.

In 1885, he had an idea that ought to make him a fortune at last: he would take a consignment of military weapons and ammunition by caravan to Choa, where he would sell them to King Menelik. He invested all his savings in the scheme and found two partners, Soleillat and Labatut. Both soon died, but Rimbaud did not give in. He left in September 1886 ('the route is very long, nearly two months' march all the way to Ankober').

Ugo Ferrandi witnessed his departure: 'He walked ahead of the caravan, always on foot ... A journey of fifty days in the most arid of deserts.' Between Tajoura and Ankober was a remote track across the dead immensity of a desert of basalt.

The sun burned savagely. The roads were 'horrible, recall-ing the presumed horror of lunar landscapes'. When he arrived, the king was not there. The expedition turned into a financial disaster. Rimbaud was exhausted and had lost everything. He returned to Harar and calmly resumed his small trading. Until his knee started hurting, and swelled enormously. He was thirty-six.

~

Arthur Rimbaud at fifteen: a frail boy with eyes of a striking and distant blue. At dawn, on the mornings of his escapes, he rose without a sound in the dark house, and closed the front door quietly behind him. And with beating heart watched the small pale roads calmly emerging from shadow. 'Let's go!' On foot. Every time on foot, and measuring with his 'unrivalled legs' the breadth of the earth.

How many times, from Charleville to Charleroi? How many times with Delahaye, in the months of war when the college was closed, to buy tobacco in Belgium? How many times returning from Paris without anything of value, belly gnawed with hunger? How many times later on the southern routes: Marseille or Italy? How many times finally along the desert roads, from Zeilah to Harar, and the 1885 expedition?

Always on foot, every time. 'I'm a pedestrian, nothing more.' Nothing more.

To walk, to make progress, anger is needed. With him there is always that parting cry, that furious joy.

Let's go, hat, greatcoat, both fists in pockets, and step outside.
Forward, route!
Let's go!

And he walked.

Anger is needed to leave, to walk. That doesn't come from outside. In the hollow of the belly the pain of being here, the impossibility of remaining where you are, of being buried alive, of simply staying. The weather is bad where you are, he wrote from the mountains of Harar. Where you are, the winters are too long and the rain too cold. But here, where we are, in Abyssinia, the misery and boredom are just as impossible, the immobility palls: nothing to read, no one to talk to, nothing to gain.

Here, it's impossible. Impossible here, for a single day more. Here, it's 'atrocious'. Time to go; 'Forward, route!' Every route is good to follow, every road towards the sun, towards more light. Doubtless it's no better elsewhere, but at least it's away from here. The route is needed, to get there. 'Fists in my ripped pockets.' In reality it is only en route, on paths, on roads, that there isn't a here.

'Adieu to here, no matter where.'

Walking as an expression of anger, of empty decision. Taking to the road always means departing: leaving behind. In departures on foot there is always something final which is lacking from other forms of transport that make it possible to turn back, where nothing is irreversible. And when you leave, you always feel this mixture of anxiety and light-heartedness. Anxious because you are abandoning something (coming back is a failure; it is impossible to come back on foot, except from a simple short stroll; but when you walk for a long time, several days, it's impossible; walking means going forward; the road is long, coming back would mean wasted hours; time is serious and weighty). But light-hearted due to all you are leaving behind; the others stay, remain on the spot, stuck. While our lightness of heart is carrying us somewhere else, trembling.

The Paris escapades, the London walks, the excursions to Belgium, the crossings of the Alps, the treks through the desert. And finally Harar, with that hideously swelling knee. 'I'm going badly at present,' he wrote on 20 January 1891. His leg hurt so much that he was unable to sleep. Inured – as he was – to suffering, he continued to work and busy himself. He struggled on. But when the leg became completely rigid he decided to leave, selling up at a loss. On 7 April he left Harar for ever, at six in the morning, on a litter. He engaged six men to carry him, taking turns. Eleven days of unrelieved suffering, including one period of sixteen hours under lashing rain: 'That did me a lot of harm.' More than 300 kilometres in eleven days, carried, shaken about, he who knew so well how to cover the ground! After a short stop to settle his affairs, another eleven days on a ship (the *Amazone*) to reach Marseille.

He was taken to the Conception hospital. 'I'm bad, very bad.' Urgent amputation was deemed necessary. They cut well above the knee. 'The doctor says I'll still be getting it for a month, and even then I will only be able to start walking again very gradually.' The cut healed correctly. 'I've ordered a wooden leg, it only weighs two kilos, it'll be ready in eight days. I'll try to walk very slowly with that.' Immobility infuriated Rimbaud. His mother came to see him at one point, then returned home. 'I would like to be doing this and that, going here and there, seeing, living, going away.' He couldn't bear the hospital any longer, and decided to return to his family in Roche, by train. Back to the starting point after twenty years. His sister Isabelle cared for him with immense devotion, ignoring his irascibility. His condition worsened nevertheless: he hardly ate, he could no longer sleep, his whole body hurt. He drank infusions of the poppy all day long.

Mere skin and bone, insubstantial as an autumn leaf, he still decided to set off again. Even summer had become too cold for him in the North. He would board a ship from Marseille and disembark at Algiers, or Aden. He was close to the end, but he wanted to leave, and he left. 'Lord, when cold is the prairie ...' Towards the sun.

On 23 August, accompanied by his sister, he took a train. Every transfer, from the house to the cart, from the cart to the train, from station to station, was a new calvary. The journey broke him completely, and he was hospitalized on arrival at Marseille.

The doctors who received him knew he was dying: they gave him a few weeks, months at most. This would be his last stop, but no one told him so. On 3 September he managed to note in a firm, unshaky hand: 'I am awaiting the artificial leg. Send it to me at once when it arrives, I am in a hurry to get away from here.'

To walk again. Every day he talked about his new leg,

he longed for it so that he might 'try to stand up, to walk'. He was in constantly increasing pain, he wept on seeing through the window a vivid blue sky, calling him to go out. As if in bitter reproach, he told his sister: 'I'll be going into the ground and you'll still be walking in the sun!' His whole body was gradually stiffening, going rigid. 'I'm just an immobile log.' He was taking morphine almost continuously, to suppress the unbearable agony. Early in November he fell into delirium. It was his final week.

Isabelle's memoirs include an account of the dying Rimbaud's last-minute conversion,* but if I had to state a preference it would strongly favour the description of his final delirium. He was confined to bed, his upper body increasingly paralysed. Soon the heart would be affected. He was hallucinating: he saw himself walking, departing once again. He was in Harar, and had to leave for Aden.

'Let's go!' How many times had he said that? The caravan had to be organized, camels found and hired. He dreamed that his prosthetic leg was a success, that he 'walked very easily'. He was running, desperate to be on his way. 'Quick, quick, fasten the valises and let's leave.' His last words: 'Quick, they're expecting us.' He complained that he shouldn't be allowed to sleep so much, for it was late. It was too late.

'Lord, when cold is the prairie.' To travel far, to flee once more the family and the mother ('la daromphe', a Rimbaud distortion of 'daronne' meaning 'old lady, mother'), to

---

* They appeared in the *Mercure de France* under the title 'Relics'.

escape the cold of the Ardennes, the freezing wind howling in the dark forests; to flee from sadness and boredom, over-cast skies, dark days, black crows too in a dark grey sky, to flee the atrocious misery of winter. To flee the sordid idiocies of the seated ones. 'Leave behind the warblers of May.'

Walking. I find in Rimbaud that sense of walking as flight. That deep joy one always feels when walking, to be leaving behind. There's no question of going back when you are walking. That's it: you've gone, departed. And the immense complementary joys of fatigue, extenuation, forgetfulness of the self and the world. All your former nar-ratives, and those tiring murmurs, drowned by the beat of your tread on the road. Exhaustion that drowns everything. You always know why you are walking: to advance, to leave, to reach, to leave again.

'Let's go, route! I'm a pedestrian, nothing more.'

Rimbaud died on 10 November 1891. He was just thirty-seven. In the deaths register of the Conception hospital, he is identified thus: 'Born in Charleville, passing through Marseille.'

Passing through. He had only gone there to leave again.

7

Solitudes

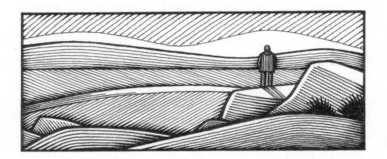

O ught one really to walk alone? Nietzsche, Thoreau and Rousseau are not alone in thinking so. Being in company forces one to jostle, hamper, walk at the wrong speed for others. When walking it's essential to find your own basic rhythm, and maintain it. The right basic rhythm is the one that suits you, so well that you don't tire and can keep it up for ten hours. But it is highly specific and exact. So that when you are forced to adjust to someone else's pace, to walk faster or slower than usual, the body follows badly.

However, complete solitude is not absolutely essential. You can be with up to three or four ... with no more than that, you can still walk without talking. Everyone walks at their own speed, slight gaps build up, and the leader can turn around from time to time, pause for a moment, call 'Everything all right?' in a detached, automatic, almost indifferent way. The reply might be a wave of the hand. Hands on hips, the others may await the slowest; then they will start again, and the order changes. The rhythms come and go, crossing one another. Going at your own pace doesn't mean walking in an absolutely uniform, regular manner; the body is not a machine. It allows itself slight relaxations or moments of affirmative joy. So with up to three or four people, walking allows these moments of shared solitude. For solitude too can be shared, like bread and daylight.

With more than four companions, the party becomes a colony, an army on the march. Shouts, whistles, people go from one to another, wait for each other, form groups which soon become clans. Everyone boasts about their equipment. When it's time to eat, they want you to 'taste this', they produce culinary treats, outbid each other ... It's hell. No longer simple or austere: a piece of society transplanted to the mountains. People start making comparisons. With five or more, it's impossible to share solitude.

So it's best to walk alone, except that one is never entirely alone. As Henry David Thoreau wrote: 'I have a great deal of company in the house, especially in the morning when nobody calls.' To be buried in Nature is perpetually distracting. Everything talks to you, greets you, demands your attention: trees, flowers, the colour of the roads. The sigh of the wind, the buzzing of insects, the babble of streams, the impact of your feet on the ground: a whole rustling murmur that responds to your presence. Rain, too. A light and gentle rain is a steady accompaniment, a murmur you listen to, with its intonations, outbursts, pauses: the distinct plopping of drops splashing on stone, the long melodious weave of sheets of rain falling steadily.

It's impossible to be alone when walking, with so many things under our gaze which are given to us through the inalienable grasp of contemplation. The intoxication of the promontory when, after a struggle, we have reached the rocky point and sat down, and when the prospect, the landscape is given to us at last. All those fields, houses, forests, paths, all ours, for us. We have mastered all that by our ascent, and it only remains to rejoice in that mastery.

Who could feel alone when he possesses the world? Seeing, dominating, looking mean possessing. But without the inconveniences of ownership: one benefits from the world's spectacle almost as a thief. But not a thief altogether: for to climb one has to work. All that I see, that is open to the gaze, is mine. As far as I can see, I possess it. Not alone: the world is mine, for me, with me.

They tell this story about a wise pilgrim: he was following a long road, under a dark stormy sky, down a valley in whose dip was a small field of ripe wheat. The well-defined field, among rough scrub and under that black sky, was a perfect square of brightness rippling gently in the wind. The pilgrim enjoyed the beautiful sight as he walked slowly along. Soon he met a peasant returning home with downcast eyes after a hard day's work, accosted him and pressed his arm, murmuring in a heartfelt tone: 'Thank you.' The peasant recoiled slightly: 'I have nothing to give you, poor man.' The pilgrim replied in a gentle voice: 'I'm not thanking you to make you give me something, but because you have already given me everything. You have cared for that square of wheat, and through your labour it has acquired the beauty it has today. Now you are only interested in the price of each grain. I've been walking, and all the way I have been nourished by its goldenness,' the old pilgrim ended with a kindly smile. The peasant turned away and walked off, shaking his head and muttering about mad people.

In that sense you aren't alone, because when walking you earn the sympathy of all the living things that surround us: trees and flowers. That is why you go walking sometimes, just to pay a visit – to green glades, groves of trees, violet-shaded valleys. You think after a few days, months or years: it's really been too long since I went there last. It's expecting me, I should go there on foot. And slowly the road, the feel of the ground underfoot, the shape of the hills, the height of the trees, all come back to you: they are acquaintances.

Lastly, you are not alone because when you walk you soon become two. Especially after walking for a long time. What I mean is that even when I am alone, there is always this dialogue between the body and the soul. When the walking is steady and continuous, I encourage, praise, congratulate: good legs, carrying me along ... almost patting my thigh, as one pats the withers of a horse. During those long moments of effort, when the body strains, I am there to support it: come on, keep it up, of course you can. When I walk, I soon become two. My body and me: a couple, an old story. Truly the soul is the body's witness. An active, vigilant witness. It must follow the other's rhythm, accompany its effort: when you press on the leg during steep ascents, when you feel its weight at the knee. You push on, and the mind punctuates each step: 'good, good, good' ... The soul is the body's pride. When I am walking I accompany myself, I am two. And that endlessly relaunched conversation can last all day without boredom. We can't walk without this split, which is how we feel ourselves making progress. When I am walking I always observe myself, egg myself on.

It sometimes happens, of course, when for example you are too deep into the rocks, overlooked by crags, no trace of vegetation – too high, too hard, tracks of pebbles and scree – that you despair a little, feel very isolated ... excluded, so to speak. It only takes the threat of a lowering black sky to render that feeling unbearable very quickly, insurmountable almost. Your throat tightens and you rush down the hard paths with anxious haste. It's impossible to walk alone for too long like that, in the crushing silence of immense blocks of stone: your own tread echoes with incredible violence. Here your breathing, moving body is a scandal, a spot of life in a cold, haughty, definitive, eternal minerality that rejects it. It happens too on days of rain or fog, when you can't see anything, and are just a body, perished with cold and advancing in the middle of nowhere.

8

Silences

Thoreau observed repeatedly that silence usually taught him more than the company of others.

Just as there are several solitudes, so there are several silences.

One always walks in silence. Once you have left streets, populated roads, public spaces (all that speed, jostling and clamour, the clatter of thousands of footsteps, the white noise of shouts and murmurs, snatches of words, the rumble and whir of engines), silence is retrieved, initially as a transparency. All is calm, expectant and at rest. You are out of the world's chatter, its corridor echoes, its muttering. Walking: it hits you at first like an immense breathing in the ears. You feel the silence as if it were a great fresh wind blowing away clouds.

There's the silence of woodland. Clumps and groves of trees form shifting, uncertain walls around us. We walk along existing paths, narrow winding strips of beaten earth. We quickly lose our sense of direction. That silence is tremulous, uneasy.

Then there's the silence of tough summer afternoon walks across the flank of a mountain, stony paths, exposed to an uncompromising sun. Blinding, mineral, shattering silence. You hear nothing but the quiet crunch of stones underfoot. An implacable, definitive silence, like a transparent death. Sky of a perfectly detached blue. You advance with eyes down, reassuring yourself sometimes with a silent mumbling. Cloudless sky, limestone slabs filled with presence: silence nothing can sidestep. Silence fulfilled, vibrant immobility, tensed like a bow.

There's the silence of early morning. For long routes in autumn you have to start very early. Outside everything is violet, the dim light slanting through red and gold leaves. It is an expectant silence. You walk softly among huge dark trees, still swathed in traces of blue night. You are almost afraid of awakening. Everything whispering quietly.

There's the silence of walks through the snow, muffled footsteps under a white sky. All around you nothing moves. Things and even time itself are iced up, frozen solid in silent immobility. Everything is stopped, unified, thickly padded. A watching silence, white, fluffy, suspended as if in parentheses.

Lastly, there's the unique silence of night. If, owing to nightfall, when the lodging is still too far, you have chosen to sleep under the stars, taken trouble to find a good place, warmed yourself and eaten, you fall asleep quickly and easily. But then there always comes that moment of awakening, after several hours of slumber, still in the fastness of the night. The eyes open abruptly as if seized by the depth of the silence. Any shifting to ease your limbs, the rustle of your sleeping bag, assume enormous proportions. So what is it that woke you? The very sound of silence?

In a chapter entitled 'A Night Among the Pines', Stevenson mentions this sudden-awakening phenomenon, placing it around two in the morning and seeing it as affecting, at the same moment, all living beings asleep outside. He views it as a minor cosmic mystery: could it be a tremor of the earth running through our bodies? A moment of acceleration in the night? An invisible dew originating in the stars? At any rate it is a startling moment, in which the silence can be heard physically as music, or rather it is the moment when, lifting your head, you hear quite distinctly the music of the spheres.

What is called 'silence' in walking is, in the first place, the abolishment of chatter, of that permanent noise that blanks and fogs everything, invading the vast prairies of our consciousness like couch-grass. Chatter deafens: it turns everything into nonsense, intoxicates you, makes you lose your head. It is always there on all sides, overflowing, running everywhere, in all directions.

But above all, silence is the dissipation of our language. Everything, in this world of work, leisure, activity, reproduction and consumption of things, everything has its function, its place, its utility, and a specific word that corresponds to it. Likewise our grammar reproduces our sequencings of action, our laborious grasp of things, our fuss and bustle. Always doing, producing, forever busying ourselves. Our language is tailored to the conventions of fabricated things, predictable gestures, normalized behaviours, received attitudes. Artifices adapted to one another: language is caught in the everyday construction of the world, participates in it, belongs to the same order of things as pictures and numbers and lists – order, injunction, synthesis, decision, report, code. Language is an instruction slip, a price list. In the silence of a walk, when you end up losing the use of words because by then you are doing nothing but walk (and here one should beware of those expedition guides who recode, detail, inform, punctuate the walk with names and explanations – the relief, the types of rock, the slopes, the names of plants and their virtues – to give the impression that everything visible has a name, that there is a grammar for everything that can be felt), in that silence you hear better, because you are finally hearing what has no vocation to be retranslated, recoded, reformatted.

'Before speaking, a man should see.'

The only words remaining to the walker are barely mutterings, words he catches himself saying ('Come on, come on, come on', 'That's it, 'Oh, all right', 'There it is, there it is'), words hung like garlands on the fleeting seconds, commonplace, words not to say anything but to punctuate the silence with a supplementary vibration, just to hear his own echo.

9

The Walker's Waking Dreams – Rousseau

I never do anything but when walking, the countryside is my study.
Jean-Jacques Rousseau, *Mon Portrait*

Rousseau claimed to be incapable of thinking properly, of composing, creating or finding inspiration except *when walking*. The mere sight of a desk and chair was enough to make him feel sick and drain him of all courage. It was during long walks that the ideas would come, on the road that sentences would spring to his lips, as a light punctuation of the movement; it was paths that stimulated his imagination.

In his writing we find three set-piece experiences of walking: dawn, midday and dusk.

He walked from sixteen to nineteen years old. Those were the long journeys of his youth, filled with exaltation and fervour. Later he was a 'Monsieur', as he put it – a man about town who went everywhere in a barouche, feverishly seeking fame and recognition.

> I have never journeyed on foot except in my younger days, and then always with the greatest pleasure. Duties, business, luggage, soon obliged me to play the gentleman and take a carriage; gnawing cares, perplexities, and discomfort got in with me, and from that moment, instead of feeling, as before, nothing but the pleasure of travelling, my only anxiety was to reach the end of my journey.

After years of masked play-acting, tiresome scheming and dodging, came the first break. He started again to take long meditative walks along forest roads or lakeside paths. He became bearish, unsociable.

Later still he became a sort of outlaw, driven out wherever he went, a leading undesirable, condemned in Paris, in Geneva. His books were publicly burned and he was threatened with jail. People threw stones at him in Moutier. He retreated from one place to another, wandered this way and that, became suspicious of his protectors. And when all the hatreds had subsided and the issues faded with time and lassitude, there would be the last walks, the crepuscular *reveries*. Although he had become an old man, he liked nothing so much as going for long walks, to kill the days. When there is really nothing left to do or believe, except to remember, walking helps retrieve the absolute simplicity of presence, beyond all hope, before any expectation.

~

As described in the Confessions, the earliest walks were long, happy, sunsoaked trips, and of fundamental significance. Due to both poverty and inclination, they involved covering immense distances on foot: from Annecy to Turin, from Soleure to Paris, then from Paris to Lyon, from Lyon finally to Chambéry.

Rousseau was just sixteen when, one March evening in 1728, he found the gates of Geneva closed on returning from a youthful escapade. He then decided not to turn up for work in the engraver's workshop the next day, for fear of the clouts he would get. As one must eat, he left to seek refuge with a Catholic curé not far away, in Savoie. After feeding him, and scolding him roundly for having been born a Calvinist, the priest sent him on to Annecy to see a pious woman who would teach him the true religious way and give him protection and comfort. The young man prepared himself on the way to humour an elderly duenna.

He saw her. She was twenty-eight (gentle gaze, angelic mouth, and the loveliest of arms): Madame de Warens. The vision transfixed him with love and desire. He had just run into love: an angel of generosity and sweetness, helpful, desirable. Alas, having just met her, he had to leave her immediately to please her: she hustled him off to Turin to convert, to renounce in Italy his Protestant faith. He promised and set off on foot, in the company of Monsieur and Madame Sabran, at a slow pace. It was going to take twenty days, given that the mountains were still covered in snow. But eventually they got across the Alps via the Mont-Cenis, feeling like Hannibal ... to the young, all is granted. 'I felt that I need not trouble further about myself; others had undertaken the charge. So I went on my way with light step, freed from this burden; youthful desires, enchanting hopes, brilliant plans filled my soul.'

Barely a year later Rousseau, having become a Catholic in Turin in the course of an eventful week, and tried his hand at the profession of flunkey, returned to his protectress. The journey was again made on foot, with a random companion (Bâcle) and in a joyously insouciant spirit. The third journey took place in 1731, after a thousand vicissitudes and some whimsical adventures. Rousseau was in Solothurn, in Switzerland; well-meaning souls there sent him to Paris, to meet a retired colonel seeking a nephew to raise in the profession of arms. The walk took a good two weeks, Rousseau fantasizing along the way of rapidly becoming a general, leading magnificent armies to glory. But the old officer was a skinflint, a miser who exploited him. Rousseau ran away, and again walked all the way to Lyon, and then to Chambéry, to find 'Maman' again. That was his last long pedestrian journey.

From the moment he had left Mme de Warens – her eyes of purest blue, delicate neck and bosom, milk-white arms – he had dreamed of her all the way, and imagined himself finding her ghosts and doubles in every wayside inn. During long, easy walks, on well-traced routes, when all you have to do is follow an interminable set of hair-pins, you hatch a thousand plans, invent a thousand tales. The body slowly advances, with measured steps, and that same tranquillity gives the mind a day off. Relieved of duty by the automatic functioning of the body, it follows up its fantasies and projects itself into a labyrinth of stories. While the gentle shock-free rolling of happy legs drives the evolving narrative forward: challenges arise, their solutions are found, fresh ambushes appear. As you follow the wide, single, clearly marked route, a thousand bifurcations swarm in your mind. The heart takes one and renounces another, then chooses a third. It wanders away, comes back.

> I was young, and in good health; I had sufficient money and abundant hopes; I travelled on foot and I travelled alone. That I should consider this an advantage would appear surprising, if the reader were not by this time familiar with my disposition. My pleasing chimeras kept me company, and never did my heated imagination give birth to any that were more magnificent. When anyone offered me an empty seat in a carriage, or accosted me on the road, I made a wry face when I saw that fortune overthrown, the edifice of which I reared during my walk.

When you are that age, when you can't say that you have loved, because love is still a future flowering that you yearn for with your entire being, there is lightness in your step, eagerness for the great love at the end of the road. Then Rousseau crossed the Alps. The prospects that opened over hillcrests, the sublime views of the peaks, seemed to endorse the maddest ambitions. What would he find at the next lodging? Who would be dining there? Everything could, everything *should* offer the opportunity for extraordinary encounters: stout-hearted companions, mysterious women, louche characters, formidable schemers. Every time you approach a hamlet, a farm, a great house, anything could happen. And when evening comes, and it's time to eat, even if the hostess is less beautiful than you might have hoped, and the innkeeper less forthcoming, you hardly notice: the body is content to fill those immense hollows gouged in the belly by the wind. Afterwards, you fall asleep in seconds to visit other dreams. That first walk is infinitely sweet ... at sixteen or even twenty you carry no burden but your cheerful hopes. No memories weigh down your shoulders. All is still possible, all is yet to be experienced. Desires are forming within you, delighted with all possibilities. It is the walk of happy daybreaks, the resplendent mornings of life.

> I have never thought so much, existed so much, lived so much, been so much myself, if I may venture to use the phrase, as in the journeys which I have made alone and on foot ... I dispose of Nature in its entirety as its lord and master; my heart, roaming from object to object, mingles and identifies itself with those which soothe it, wraps itself up in charming fancies, and is intoxicated with delicious sensations.

Rousseau was now past forty. He had already done a lot: embassy secretary in Venice, music teacher, encyclopaedist ... He had made friends, enemies, a reputation; his name was often mentioned. He had schemed, written, invented, sought glory and recognition. Now he suddenly decided to stop frequenting society, to give up haunting learned and distinguished circles, to cease pursuing a success that he found slow in coming, and in whose very prospect he was already losing interest. He abandoned wigs and fine clothes, deserted the salons, resigned from all high-profile posts. Soon he was dressed like a poor man, and copying music sheets for a living. Because he wanted (as he kept saying) to rely only on himself. He was spoken of as a new Diogenes: Rousseau was the 'doggish man' of the Enlightenment.

But the break wasn't a clean or abrupt one. At the same time the king discovered his music, took a fancy to it, and made the fact known. Also at the same moment, his *Discours sur les arts* was being read and talked about everywhere. And he was still intending to defend his views on French music.

Increasingly, nevertheless, he longed for one thing above all: to remain alone for a long time, to leave Paris, bury himself in the woods. He had already written that culture, letters and learning had helped make humanity decadent, rather than completing it. With the thinkers of the time, all around him, chorusing the songs of liberation through reason, perfectibility through education and progress through science, he aspired to show that society corrupts mankind. But when he wrote that in his first *Discours*, it was from a desire for glory; and his whole life reveals a single-minded wish to be known, recognized, loved and applauded.

Past forty, it's time to draw a line under social quests, celebrity friendships, whirling fashions and incessant tittle-tattle. Rousseau no longer wanted anything but forest paths. To be alone, far from the hubbub. No longer to have to check his social share price daily, calculate his friends, ration his enemies, flatter his protectors, ceaselessly measure his importance in the eyes of fops and imbeciles, return looks in kind, avenge words with words. He wanted to be elsewhere, far away: buried in the woods, where there would be deep silent nights, transparent mornings. To achieve that, he needed to make himself detestable to many. But he knew how to set about it: he would arrange his life so that he no longer had to run or crawl, but could walk.

This was also the time when he was writing a second *Discourse: On the Origin and Basis of Inequality Among Men*. He would go out in the morning and plunge into the forests of Saint-Germain or the Bois de Boulogne. The November of 1753 was exceptionally fine and mild, deep soft autumnal blue skies, the rustle of fallen leaves, golden and russet colours. To do what exactly? Walk, work, discover. Immense solitary walks, regular, daily. Trampling the earth with his heavy shoes, disappearing into the brush, wandering among ancient trees.

Alone, and surrounded – or rather filled – with the quiet murmur of animals and trees, the sigh of wind through the leaves, the rattle and creak of branches. Alone, and fulfilled. Because now he could breathe, breathe and surrender to a well-being slow as a forest path, without any thrill of pleasure but absolutely peaceful. A lukewarm happiness, persistent as a monotonous day: happiness just to be there, to feel the rays of a winter sun on his face and hear the muffled creaking of the forest. Walking there, Rousseau listened: to the leaping of his heart, no longer assailed by worldly emotions, a heart no longer affected by society's desires, but surrendered at last to its primary, natural beat.

And there, walking all day long, Rousseau conceived the insane plan to identify – in himself, *homo viator*, walking man – the natural man, one not disfigured by culture, education, art: man as he would have been before books or salons, before society or paid labour.

He wasn't walking to find his own identity, or to rediscover a disguised singularity, or to get a rest from shuffling masks; but walking long distances to find in himself the man from another age, the first man. Walking, but not as one might go to the desert to escape the world and its horrors, purified by solitude, prepared for one's celestial destiny. But walking to find in himself the man fresh from the hands of Nature, the absolute primitive. So he walked at great length, going far, into the real wilds, endlessly turning over the question: what is it that *resists* in me, what in me is the exact contemporary of the gravity of the trees, the uneasy brother of these beasts whose rustlings I perceive? What can I find in myself that is *natural*, what can I discover that isn't in books but that I can only find by walking in solitude?

Find the contours of the first man, the absolute savage; scrape off, with the slow wear of these forest walks, the social man's varnish, revealing the portrait which isn't in books because they are only about recent man, civilized, denatured, swollen with social passions: draw that first man.

And thus discover, through endless solitary walks, desolate, far from the world, in the sole company of trees and beasts, rediscover in oneself the first man.

> The remainder of the day, I buried myself in the forest, where I sought and found the picture of those primitive times, of which I boldly sketched the history. I demolished the pitiful lies of mankind; I dared to expose their nature in all its nakedness, to follow the progress of time and of the things which have disfigured this nature; and, comparing the man, as man has made him, with the natural man, I showed him, in his pretended perfection, the true source of his misery.

And while pursuing this rather improbable research, which required long days of trudging through forests rather than through books, Rousseau's relentless self-examination did result in the internal appearance of a frail, wavering image of primitive, wild, innocent man. And as that ghostly image gradually took shape – he imagined it as a furtive shadow slipping behind the oaks – he perceived it not as fierce or brutish, ruled by disordered impulses and violent instincts, but rather as timid, absolutely adjusted to a motherly, enveloping Nature, and essentially solitary and happy. For the fullness, the simple well-being experienced there by Rousseau, purged of the exhausting artificial passions that rule the social world, when walking alone, must also be the feeling experienced by the first man in the timeless flow of 'peaceful and innocent days'. And how much more intense that well-being was than the phoney excitements, the idiot satisfactions and vain joys of the world!

In the midst of so much philosophy, humanity, and polite-
ness, and so many sublime maxims, we have nothing to show
for ourselves but a deceitful and frivolous exterior, honour
without virtue, reason without wisdom, and pleasure without
happiness.

Thus the walker came to see the whole of human history,
with its changes and struggles, in the form of a steady, vertiginous decline. And to see civilized man with his civility
and hypocrisy, filled with malice and envy, as the real brute
beast. To see the social world with its injustice and violence,
its inequalities and miseries, and the states with their armies
and police forces, as the real jungles. To see social man as
filled with rancour, hatred, jealousy and resentment.

And when the solitary walker tried to unearth from
under layers of culture the inborn truth of human passions,
he only discovered a naïve and unassuming self-love (very
remote from egotism or touchy self-esteem, which are ways
of favouring oneself; but favour is always the opposite of
love), in other words an instinctive inclination to take an
interest in himself, to preserve himself and pay attention to
his well-being. So the natural man instinctively *loves himself*,
but never favours himself. Only in society do you learn to do
that. And you have to walk a long way to relearn self-love.

Alone at last, having purged his heart of all stupid passions and dropped his masks along meandering footpaths,
Rousseau also started to feel a pure, transparent, limitless
compassion growing within him. Those long hours of
walking drained away envies and grudges, in a similar way
to bereavement or immense misfortune: the old hatreds

suddenly appeared vain, petty, futile. Which does not mean you are suddenly ready to love your former enemies and embrace them. Such loving reconciliations are of the same stuff, painted on the same canvas, as stubborn hatreds. But when you walk, it's different: you no longer feel anything for the other, neither bitter aggression nor gushing fraternity. Merely a neutral availability, taking on colour when another is found in tears. Then through natural compassion the heart opens, dilates spontaneously before the apparent pain, like petals opening to light. And you go to their aid, you long to help with all your heart.

> There is besides another principle that has escaped Hobbes, and which, having been given to man to moderate, on certain occasions, the blind and impetuous sallies of self-love, or the desire of self-preservation previous to the appearance of that passion, allays the ardour, with which he naturally pursues his private welfare, by an innate abhorrence to see beings suffer that resemble him.

Spite, suspicion and hatred aren't, therefore, rooted in primary savagery: they were grafted onto us, locked as we are in the world's artificial garden, and have never stopped burgeoning and developing to stifle our naturally compassionate heart.

That was the discovery of those open-ended walks through the undergrowth, following wandering paths; losing yourself the better to hear your heart, to feel the first man palpitating within you. You come out of that better adjusted to yourself: you no longer worship yourself, you simply love yourself. You come out of it better adjusted to others: you no longer detest them, you sincerely pity them. In the end, from those paths bathed in the tranquillity of a tired sun, the gentleness of dead leaves circling to the ground, the deep slow natural breathing, from there the civilized world, society with its fears, its tinpot grandiloquence, its electric thrills, its furies: all that, seen from down there, from behind the sweet barrier of trees, seems nothing more than one long-drawn-out disaster.

~

Nightfall. Rousseau was now nearly sixty years old. He had become an outcast, rejected by all, proscribed everywhere, in republican Geneva as well as monarchist France. He made a pathetic attempt to become an exile in England, but created far too many enemies there. For a long time he wandered here and there, half in hiding, and several times considered having himself jailed to sample peaceful prison walls. And then came the long, slow moment when he *gave way*.

He gave it all up. Those were his last walks: he returned to Paris, drained of courage, unwilling to fight on. And there he was forgotten, little by little, as society's focus moved on to other things, other hatreds. And that was that.

I am referring to the last walks, the ones that punctuate the book *Reveries*, or rather the ones that can be discerned in it, far beyond books. I am talking about those undefined walks, not undertaken to *prepare* for anything, not seen as an opportunity to *find* new words (new defences, new identities, new ideas). The walks one imagines at Ermenonville, the last ones in May and June 1778. There is no longer even the act of walking as a method, a heuristic and a projection. Walking is no longer undertaken to fuel invention, but exactly for *nothing*: just to connect with the movement of the sinking sun, to echo with slow tread the cadence of the minutes, hours and days. To walk like that is to punctuate the day a little, without really thinking about it, as one's fingers unconsciously tap out the beat of a tune on a table-top. Essentially a matter of no longer expecting anything, letting time come, surrendering to the floodtide of days and the exhaustion of nights. Well-being in that context requires a uniform and moderate movement, without either shocks or pauses. Walking thus means accompanying time, match-ing its pace as one does with a child.

Then, during those long crepuscular walks, forgot-ten memories, welcome as old friends, rise to the surface of the conscious mind. Memories for which one at last feels indulgence. They no longer wound by reawakening painful episodes, or fatigue the soul with yearning for a lost happiness. They come floating up like aquatic flowers, dif-fering only in their shifting colours and shapes. Indifferent, smiling, meaningful only in the vague, amusing, detached certainty of having once experienced them ... Was that really me, that dreamy child, that young man intoxicated by worldliness?

Rousseau had once been able to say that while walking he was master of his imaginings, having to come to terms only with his visions, absolutely certain of his dreams. The last walks by contrast have the immense gentleness of detachment, a letting go, with nothing left to hope for or expect. Just life, allowing yourself to exist. Because there's no need to be anyone, you can just succumb to the passage of a current, or rather to that persistent rivulet of existence.

That gives the returning memories a fraternal aspect, like timeworn, familiar old brothers. And for our own good we become that old brother, the one we love for the sole reason that he has *been through the mill*. In this way, in these walks, you conceive an affection for yourself. You forgive yourself, instead of making excuses. Nothing left to lose, just keep walking. And everything, all around, takes on this new face: indulgence for the fearful, hiding bird, for the fragile, wilting flower, indulgence for the thick foliage. For, once you no longer expect anything from the world on these aimless and peaceful walks, that is when the world delivers itself to you, gives itself, yields itself up. When you no longer expect anything. All is then bestowed as a supplement, a gratuitous favour of presence, of being there. You are already dead to the world of struggles, triumphs, projects, hopes. But this sun, these colours, that scroll of blue smoke gently rising down there, these crackling branches: everything is given and more. It's a gift. Identities, histories, written accounts, consumed, avenged, repeated, all that is behind you. All over. But everything is given as well: the spring sunshine of 1778, the glitter on the Valois lakes, the velvety Ermenonville green.

The *Reveries* enable us to imagine the last walks in June, in a state of marvellous contentment: walking long after what had been achieved, as a relaxation of Being. Destinies had been completed, closed, wrapped up. The books had shut. He didn't have to be Rousseau any more, or Jean-Jacques, or for or against anything or anyone. But just a vibration among the trees and stones, on the paths. Walking to breathe in the landscape. Every step an inspiration born to die immediately, well beyond the oeuvre.

> I like to walk at my ease, and to stop when I like. A wandering life is what I want. To walk through a beautiful country in fine weather, without being obliged to hurry, and with a pleasant prospect at the end, is of all kinds of life the one most suited to my taste.

10

Eternities

We must really manage one day to do without 'news'. Reading the newspapers in fact only tells us what we didn't yet know. And that is exactly what we are looking for: something new. But what we didn't yet know is exactly what we forget immediately. Because as soon as we know it, we have to leave room for what we don't yet know, which will come tomorrow. Newspapers have no memory: one piece of news drives out another, each event displaces another which sinks without a trace. Rumours bulge up, then suddenly subside. One juicy 'I have it on the best authority' succeeds another in a shapeless, perpetual cascade.

When you walk, news becomes unimportant. Soon you

have lost all knowledge of the world and its gymnastics, the most recent own goal, the latest scandal. You no longer await the surprise development, or want to hear how it really all began, or what happened in the end. Heard the latest? When you are walking, all that ceases to matter. Being in the presence of what absolutely endures detaches us from that ephemeral news for which we are usually agog. After walking far and long, you can even come to wonder in surprise how you could ever have been interested in it. The slow respiration of things makes everyday huffing and puffing appear vain, unhealthy agitation.

The first eternity we encounter is that of rocks, of the swooping contour of the plains, of the skylines: all that is *resistant*, unchanging. And being confronted with that overhanging solidity reduces trivial facts, the pathetic news, to the significance of dust blowing in the wind. A motionless eternity vibrating where it stands. Walking is to experience these quietly and humbly insistent realities – the tree growing between rocks, the watchful bird, the streamlet finding its course – without expecting anything. Walking makes the rumours and complaints fall suddenly silent, stops the ceaseless interior chatter through which we comment on others, evaluate ourselves, recompose, interpret. Walking shuts down the sporadic soliloquy to whose surface sour rancours, imbecile satisfactions and easy imaginary vengeances rise sluggishly in turn. You are facing a mountain, walking among great trees, and you think: they are just there. They are there, they didn't expect me, they were always there. They were there long before me and they will still be there long after me.

A day will surely come when we will just stop worrying, stop being taken over and imprisoned by our chores (while knowing very well that we have invented most of them, imposed them on ourselves). Working: accumulating savings, perpetual anxiety not to miss any career opportunity, coveting this or that job, rushing the work, worrying about competitors. Do this, take a look at that, invite so-and-so: social constraints, cultural fashions, busy busy busy ... but always to do something, not to 'be'. We leave that for later: there's always something better, more urgent, more important to be done now. Being can wait until tomorrow. But tomorrow brings chores for the day after ... An endless tunnel. And they call it living. So pervasive is the pressure that even leisure carries the stamp of single-mindedness: sport carried to painful extremes, stimulant relaxations, costly dinners, active nights, expensive holidays. Until finally the only way out seems to be through melancholia or death.

You're doing nothing when you walk, nothing but walking. But having nothing to do but walk makes it possible to recover the pure sensation of being, to rediscover the simple joy of existing, the joy that permeates the whole of childhood. So that walking, by unburdening us, prising us from the obsession with doing, puts us in touch with that childhood eternity once again. I mean that walking is so to speak child's play. To marvel at the beauty of the day, the brightness of the sun, the grandeur of the trees, the blue of the sky: to do that takes no experience, no ability. It is therefore sensible, incidentally, to distrust people who walk too much and too far: they have already seen everything and only make comparisons. The eternal child is one who has never seen anything so beautiful, because he doesn't compare. So when we set off for a few days, a few weeks, we are not just leaving behind our jobs, neighbours, affairs, habits and troubles; but also our complicated identities, our faces and masks. None of that can hold for long, because walking never calls for anything but the body. None of your knowledge, your reading, your connections will be of any use here: two legs suffice, and big eyes to see with. Walk alone, across mountains or through forests.

You are nobody to the hills or the thick boughs heavy with greenery. You are no longer a role, or a status, not even an individual, but a body, a body that feels sharp stones on the paths, the caress of long grass and the freshness of the wind. When you walk, the world has neither present nor future: nothing but the cycle of mornings and evenings. Always the same thing to do all day: walk. But the walker who marvels while walking (the blue of the rocks in a July evening light, the silvery green of olive leaves at noon, the violet morning hills) has no past, no plans, no experience. He has within him the eternal child. While walking I am but a simple gaze. Emerson wrote:

> I am glad to the brink of fear. In the woods too, a man casts off his years, as the snake his slough, and at what period soever of life, is always a child. In the woods, is perpetual youth. ... There I feel that nothing can befall me in life – no disgrace, no calamity (leaving me my eyes) which nature cannot repair.

> Standing on the bare ground – my head bathed by the blithe
> air, and uplifted into infinite space – all mean egotism van-
> ishes. I become a transparent eye-ball; I am nothing; I see all ...

With its great shocks, Nature thus awakens us from the human nightmare.

Perhaps yet another, the eternity of consonance. You would have to describe exactly what aspect of a landscape comes to you when walking that couldn't come in any other way. As a car passenger, watching the landscapes pass, I contemplate pure mountain skylines, am transported across fascinating deserts, wind through incredible forests. From time to time I ask to stop, stretch my legs, take a few photos. Things are pointed out and details given: what species of tree, prevailing plant life, the back of those outcrops. Of course the sun is also hot, the colours vivid too, and the sky generous.

But walking causes absorption. Walking interminably, taking in through your pores the height of the mountains when you are confronting them at length, breathing in the shape of the hills for hours at a time during a slow descent. The body becomes steeped in the earth it treads. And thus, gradually, it stops being in the landscape: it *becomes* the landscape. That doesn't have to mean dissolution, as if the walker were fading away to become a mere inflection, a footnote. It's more a flashing moment: sudden flame, time catching fire. And here, the feeling of eternity is all at once that vibration between presences. Eternity, here, in a spark.

11

Conquest of the
Wilderness – Thoreau

David Henry Thoreau was born in the small town of Concord, Mass., near Boston, in July 1817, the third child of a pencil manufacturer. He did well at Harvard, and after graduating started teaching at a high school, but stayed there barely a fortnight. He objected to the use of corporal punishment on his pupils, and wanted his lessons to alternate with long walks. He returned to the family pencil factory. In 1837 he reversed the order of his given names, becoming Henry David Thoreau, and started writing a journal which he kept for the rest of his life.

In 1838 he founded a private school with his brother, but the experiment did not last long. He was soon working as a factotum in Emerson's household, while publishing poems in *The Dial*, frequenting the town's Transcendentalist Club and helping to edit its review. He left Concord for a time to act as tutor to Emerson's nephews in Staten Island, NY, but stayed there only a year. In March 1845 he started building a cabin near Walden Pond, where Emerson had bought a piece of land. It was to be his philosophic act.

He lived there alone for more than two years, in perfect autarchy, among trees, beside a lake, tilling the soil, walking, reading and writing. In July 1846 he was arrested at the cabin and taken to jail for refusing to pay his poll tax arrears, in protest against the Mexican–American war and the government's failure to abolish slavery. The experience led eventually to a major and influential political work, *Civil Disobedience*. But he only spent one night in jail because a benefactor – his aunt, it is thought – paid the tax against his wishes.

He left Walden in July 1847 and lived in the Emerson household for a year, then returned to his family home, now working as a land surveyor. He made a number of trips – to Quebec, New Hampshire and to the White Mountains, where he made contact with Indian tribes. He continued to campaign for the abolition of slavery.

Thoreau died of tuberculosis at the age of forty-four, leaving an immense, fascinating oeuvre including the magical *Walden*, the distilled account of his two years living in the forest. He is the author of the first philosophic treatise on walking: *Walking*.

Thoreau lived in the first half of the nineteenth century,

at the beginning of the era of large-scale mass production (soon to evolve into all-devouring big capitalism and industrial exploitation – of workers, but also of resources). He foresaw the single-minded scramble for profits, and the vandalism of a Nature being treated as a free source of lucre. Confronted with the development of this lust for unlimited wealth, faced with the blind capitalization of material goods, Thoreau proposed a *new economics*.

The principle is a simple one. Instead of asking what return a given activity will produce, the question is what it costs in terms of pure life: 'the cost of a thing is the amount of what I will call life which is required to be exchanged for it, immediately or in the long run.' This is also a way of distinguishing between profit and benefit. What profit is obtained from a long forest walk? None: nothing saleable is produced, no social service is rendered which needs to be rewarded. In that respect, walking is thoroughly useless and sterile. In traditional economic terms it is time wasted, frittered away, dead time in which no wealth is produced. Nevertheless the benefit to me, to my life – I won't even say interior, I mean to the totality, in absolute terms – is immense: a long moment in which I look into myself, without being invaded by volatile, deafening hassles or alienated by the incessant cackle of chatterers. I capitalize myself with myself all day: a long moment in which I remain listening or in contemplation: and thus, Nature lavishes all its colours on me. On me alone. Walking magnifies receptiveness: I'm always receiving pure presence by the ton. All of that must obviously count for something. In the end walking has been the more beneficial for being less profitable: what was given to me was given in profusion.

The difference between profit and benefit is that operations producing profit can be carried out by another in my place: he would make the profit, unless he was acting on my behalf. But the fact remains that profitable activity can always be carried out by someone else. Hence the principle of competition. On the other hand, what is beneficial to me depends on gestures, acts, living moments which it would be impossible for me to delegate. Thoreau wrote in a letter that when considering a course of action, one should ask: 'Could someone else do it in my place?' If the answer is yes, abandon the idea, unless it is absolutely essential. But it is still not bound up in the inevitable part of life. Living, in the deepest sense, is something no one else can do for us. You can be replaced at work, but not for walking. That's the great difference.

The striking thing with Thoreau is not the actual content of the argument. After all, sages in earliest Antiquity had already proclaimed their contempt for possessions and trumpeted the value of spiritual riches, or again had asserted that a man is wealthy who feels that he lacks for nothing. What impresses is the form of the argument. For Thoreau's obsession with calculation runs deep. He does not say: let us reject economic weighing of quantities in favour of a pure idea of quality. He says: keep calculating, keep weighing. What exactly do I gain, or lose? What do I lose in pure living when I strive to earn more money? What it costs rich people to be rich, working, worrying, watching, never letting go.

You need a roof, Thoreau admits, walls, a bed, chairs. But: what roof, what things exactly? If you want a very large house and shiny door handles, you will have to work hard, to forget for many years what the weather is like and the colour of the sky. A lot of profit, then, which will be beneficial to no one. A roof, just to keep out the weather and the cold, three chairs (one to sit on, the second for friendship, and the third for society), one bed and a good blanket for sleeping: to have all this doesn't cost much, requires minimum labour (a little manual work, growing some beans to exchange for rice) and returns a lot: with the rest of the time, you can take very long walks – three or four hours a day – to gratify the body, and enjoy Nature's endless free spectacles (animals, the play of light slanting through the woods, depths of blue on the lake surface).

The reckoning was established, almost inverting the rhythm of the laborious, religious week: to make enough to live simply, one day's work a week is sufficient. All the other days worked are to earn the useless, the futile, the luxurious, and they devour the essential. My house, said Thoreau, who kept precise accounts, will have cost me just over twenty-eight dollars.

Work produces wealth as much as it produces poverty. Poverty in this sense is not the opposite of wealth: it is its exact complement. The rich man greedily consumes, eyeing his neighbour's plate to see if it contains more than his. The poor man for his part seizes the leftovers from the feast. They are playing the same game, it's just that there are winners and losers. The frugality Thoreau recommends is opposed as much to wealth as it is to poverty: the wealth of those who become alienated in order to have more and more, the poverty of those who toil to earn the square root of nothing. Instead it is against the system, a matter of refusing to play. Not hanging onto your capital, saving parsimoniously, refraining from spending, but staying out of the game altogether: a chosen, conscious frugality.

Frugality is not quite the same as austerity. What I mean is that austerity always includes the idea of resisting the temptation of excess: too much food, too much wealth, too many possessions, too much pleasure. Austerity pinpoints the slope from pleasure towards excess. So it is a question of holding back, cutting down on quantities, saying no. In austerity there is a good proportion of severity, a contempt or rather a fear of pleasure. Austerity is a refusal to let go, an interdiction on feeling too much for fear of being carried away. Frugality, in contrast, is the discovery that simplicity is fulfilling, the discovery of perfect enjoyment with little or nothing: water, a fruit, the breathing of the wind. Ah! To be able to get drunk, Thoreau writes, on the air we breathe!

Telling us what a lot of effort it costs a man to acquire possessions and wealth, Thoreau invites us to look at him striving day after day, and think what he denies himself by working. You should persist in calculating, and you will have to confess, Thoreau says, that you go faster on foot. Because to own a team, a carriage, will cost you days of work. The distance you can cover in a carriage in a day will cost you several months of work ... so walk! You will get there sooner, and you will also have gained the depth of the sky and the colour of the trees.

What he saw, Thoreau wrote, he made his own: he meant that one stores when walking vivid feelings and sunny memories, for the winter evenings. Our treasure, our real property, is the quantity of representations that we have taken in and conserved.

But *it is still easier to acquire wealth than to get rid of it*. The property owner's soul becomes encrusted, encysted, calloused from rubbing against material goods, while the heart of the poor man contracts with envy and rage at not having them. The rich man soon finds it very painful to be deprived of comfort – the hard wooden chair instead of the soft sofa, the impossibility of sleeping in the cold, the fatigue of walking 500 yards. As for the poor man, he remains the prisoner of his wishes for prosperity, and continues to believe in wealth.

No, really, wealth costs far too many people far too much.

Thoreau, that heroic walker – three to five hours every day – was anything but a great traveller. He did undertake a few long excursions in the forests of Maine, in Quebec and New Hampshire. But the experience of walking he writes about, which nourishes his discourse, never concerns anything but his long daily strolls around Concord, setting off from home, hands in pockets. A small-time adventurer, one might think ... but in reality he is warning us against the danger of exoticism. You see so many people who strike out far afield to recount their adventures 'out there': the necessarily fabulous encounters, the compulsory epic events, the invariably sublime landscapes, the obviously amazing food.

Performances every time, then: in narrative, in adventure, in the extreme. And yet, Thoreau's *Walden* would fascinate people more than all the travellers' tales ever told. There is a palpable radicalism in the conversion that makes those grandiloquent extreme-adventurers' epics seem dull. It cannot be said too often: there's no need to go far to walk. The true direction of walking is not towards otherness (other worlds, other faces, other cultures, other civilizations); it is towards the edge of civilized worlds, whatever they may be. Walking is setting oneself apart: at the edge of those who work, at the edges of high-speed roads, at the edge of the producers of profit and poverty, exploiters, labourers, and at the edge of those serious people who always have something better to do than receive the pale gentleness of a winter sun or the freshness of a spring breeze.

Walking is a matter not just of truth, but also of reality. To walk is to experience the real. Not reality as pure physical exteriority or as what might count as a subject, but reality as what holds good: the principle of solidity, of resistance. When you walk you prove it with every step: the earth holds good. With every pace, the entire weight of my body finds support and rebounds, takes a spring. There is everywhere a solid base somewhere underfoot.

Always when climbing, you have to make sure of your footing: there's always an imperceptible moment when you press down, to feel whether the ground resists. Then, with confidence, you place your whole body-weight on one foot, before putting down the other which had advanced through the air. What makes the legs tremble is a snow-covered path, where the sinking foot may find ice beneath; or again soil that is too dried-out, stony or sandy, where the body is forced to support itself continuously, to drag itself upward. So one shouldn't walk, but rather dance. The softness of soil irritates the foot, worries it. Inversely, paved surfaces are too hard: they resound like drums, they send the impact of each pace up through the body, when earth would absorb and swallow it. The perfect evenness of tarred roads ends by boring the foot: reality is not so monotonous.

Some decide to devote the same amount of time to writing as to reading. Thoreau, Emerson recalls, had made it a principle to give no more time to writing than he had to walking. To avoid the pitfalls of culture and libraries; for otherwise, what one writes is filled with the writing of others. For all that those others in turn had written on the books of yet others ... Writing ought to be this: testimony to a wordless, living experience. Not the commentary on another book, not the exegesis of another text. The book as witness ... but witness in the sense of the baton in a relay race.* Thus does the book, born out of experience, refer to that experience. Books are not to teach us how to live (that is the sad task of lesson-givers), but to make us want to live, to live *differently*: to find in ourselves the possibility of life, its principle. Life is uninspiring between two books (going through the monotonous, necessary, everyday motions between two readings), but the book raises the hope of a

---

* The French word *témoin*, meaning witness, has the subsidiary meaning of baton passed between runners in a relay race [translator's note].

different existence. So it shouldn't be what enables us to escape the greyness of everyday life (the everyday is life as something repeated, as the *Same*), but what enables us to pass from one life to *another*.

'How vain it is to sit down to write when you have not stood up to live.'

This writing of reality has to be sought: by only writing in the aftermath of those solidly marked, hammered paces. Because then, in thought too, one seeks only what is solid. By that I mean: write only what has been lived, intensely. Make experience your only solid foundation.

> Let us settle ourselves, and work and wedge our feet downwards through the mud and slush of opinion and tradition, and pride and prejudice, appearance and delusion, through the alluvium which covers the globe, through poetry and philosophy and religion, through church and state, through Paris and London, through New York and Boston and Concord, till we come to a hard bottom that rocks in place which we can call reality and say, 'This is and no mistake.'

Reality when you are walking is not only the solidity of the earth underfoot, but a test of your own firmness. Thoreau insists repeatedly that when walking, it is also his *own* reality that is at issue. Because a man then feels that he is *natural*, rather than *in Nature*. There is no suggestion here of 'communion' or 'fusion'. Those expressions are better suited to big mystical experiences, in which thought is simultaneously completed and wiped out in a vision of Totality. No, walking gives you *participation*: feeling the vegetable, mineral and animal aspects in yourself. I feel made from the same wood as the tree whose bark I touch in passing, the same tissue as the tall grasses I brush against, and my heavy breathing, when I stop, matches the panting of the hare that stops suddenly before me.

That reality test maintained all day long, through the solidity of the ground, but also through the consistency of my own being echoed in the profusion surrounding me, results in my own case in an abundance of confidence. Walking, as they say, 'empties the mind'. In another way, walking *fills* the mind with a different sense of purpose. Not connected with ideas or doctrines, not in the sense of a head full of phrases, quotations, theories: but full of the world's presence. That presence which, during the walk, in successive strata, has been deposited in the soul throughout the day.

And when evening comes, one hardly needs to think: just breathe, close your eyes and feel on your body the layers of landscape dissolving and recomposing ... The colour of the sky, the flash of leaves, the outlines of the jumbled hills. What may be called confidence here is not solid and hopeful, but rather a quiet certainty. Thus the man who walks all day has become certain by nightfall.

That confidence also has its source in the energies of morning. Thoreau, in all his work, wants to believe in mornings, or rather: it's the morning that instils belief. You must always start at dawn when you walk, to accompany the awakening day. And in that undecided blue hour or so, you feel as it were the first unformed babblings of presence. Walking in the morning confronts us with the

97

poverty of our wishes, in the sense that wishing is the opposite of accompaniment. I mean that following a rising morning, step by step, is anything but a sudden extraction, a brutal reversal, or a decision. The facts of daytime emerge slowly. Soon the sun will rise and everything will begin. The harshness of voluntary, solemn, talkative conversions betrays their fragility. Daytime never starts with an act of will: it arises in unworried certainty. To walk in the early morning is to understand the strength of natural beginnings.

> Love of the morning is a measure of health. But consider: let me have a draught of undiluted morning air. Morning air! If men will not drink of this at the fountainhead of the day, why, then, we must even bottle up some and sell it in the shops, for the benefit of those who have lost their subscription ticket to morning time in this world.

Thoreau's love of mornings is reflected in his exaltation of springtime, when he recounts for example how in April, the ice on Walden Pond melts and disintegrates with the pressure of new energies, how ways open and routes are invented on the river. But most of all, what he finds on some mornings and in every spring is the principle of renewal of the eternal.

'The year beginning with younger hope than ever!'

The eternal youthfulness of true hope comes from not being subjected to any condition, any verification, any test: from knowing that there is more in the form of hopefulness than in its content. Because hopefulness, basically, is a matter of belief rather than knowledge. To believe, to hope, to dream, beyond any achievement, any lesson, any past. Nature has no history: its memory goes back a year and no further. What Thoreau calls the experience of springtime is that of being swept away in the current of a pure affirmation, a wild thrust, in which nothing counts but wanting to live. Another experience, as he says, of innocence: everything recommences, everything sets off once more, and the dawn banishes the past along with the night.

'In a pleasant spring morning all men's sins are forgiven.'

When you are walking in the springtime, or at dawn, you are watchful, alert, mind stretched towards the rising day, and nothing matters but that slow affirmation. The walker has no history either, that baggage too heavy for the journey. When you walk in the morning, you have no memory. Only the joyous confidence that day will pierce the foliage of night.

'The sun is but a morning star.'

Among the sources of morning, we find the West. The East is where our memory resides: the East is culture and books, history and old defeats. There is nothing to be learned from the past, because learning from that means repeating former errors. That is why one shouldn't put one's trust in old people, or settle for their so-called experience which is nothing but the weighty mass of their repeated mistakes. One should trust only confidence itself: youth. The sources of the future lie in the West.

'We go eastward to realize history, and study the works of art and literature, retracing the steps of the race, – we go westward as into the future, with a spirit of enterprise and adventure.'

The West is a lode, the preparation of the future, a resource of being, the unopened, the ever new. But the West is also *The Wild*. The Wild is unexploited, virgin Nature, a primary, inhuman force (and non-academic: few poets, Thoreau says, know how to depict 'the west side of the mountains'), but it is also the undaunted, rebellious part of us, the part that hasn't given up on living: pure affirmation. When Emerson wrote of Thoreau that he was the most American of Americans, perhaps that is what he meant: the fascination with a primitive wilderness that can be the source of the future. The future lies in the West, Thoreau says: he can only get moving, open himself, become possible again after an immersion in the wilderness, a confrontation with it. Perhaps that is the difference between the American utopia and European musings on the wilderness. To us Europeans, the wilderness is associated with origins: an immemorial fault, permanently open, an obscure starting point. It's the ancestral place to which we may want to return, which sometimes comes up at us, but is our definitive past. For Thoreau the American, the wilderness is located in the West, before him. It is the possibility of the future. The wilderness is not the night of European memory, but the morning of the world and of humanity.

'The West of which I speak is but another name for the Wild; and what I have been preparing to say is, that in Wildness is the preservation of the world.'

That is why walking leads to a total loss of interest in

what is called – laughably no doubt – the 'news', one of whose main features is that it becomes old as soon as it is uttered. Once caught in the rhythm, Thoreau says, you are on the treadmill: you want to know what comes next. The real challenge, though, is not to know what has changed, but to get closer to what remains *eternally new*. So you should replace reading the morning papers with a walk. News items replace one another, become mixed up together, are repeated and forgotten. But the truth is that as soon as you start walking, all that noise, all those rumours, fade out. What's new? Nothing: the calm eternity of things, endlessly renewed.

The life Thoreau led – a life of resistance (Emerson recounts that his first response to any request was to say no, that he always found it easier to refuse than to assent), but also of radical choices: working only for what was necessary, walking daily at length, avoiding entanglement in the social game – was quickly judged by others (the upright, the hard-working, the propertied) to be pretty peculiar. However, it was combined with a quest for truth and authenticity. Seeking truth means going beyond appearances. It means denouncing manners and mores, traditions, the everyday, as so many conventions, hypocrisies and lies.

'Rather than love, than money, than fame, give me truth.'

A true life is always another life, a different life. Truth brings rupture, it lies to the West: to reinvent ourselves, we must find within us, under the pack-ice of received certainties and immobile opinions, the current of the wild, the one that wells up, escapes, overflows. We are prisoners of ourselves. People talk of the tyranny of public opinion, but that is nothing, Thoreau says, compared to personal opinion. We are shackled by our own judgements. Thoreau walked (towards the West, but one always heads westward when walking properly) not to find himself, but always to be in a position to reinvent himself.

It is said that at the end of Thoreau's life, a priest visited his deathbed to bring him the solace of religion by evoking the other world, the beyond. Thoreau, summoning a weak smile, is said to have replied: 'My friend, one world at a time.'

12

Energy

I n his essay *A Winter Walk*, Thoreau depicted the cold-weather walker. When you go out, he wrote, on a freezing morning – snow-covered paths and roads, trees on all sides extending bare snow-outlined branches – moving through that immense muffled frozen landscape, then you walk quickly and well, to keep warm by feeling the heat of your own body. The well-being in walking in the cold is partly from that feeling of a small stove burning in your vitals.

> There is a slumbering subterranean fire in nature which never goes out, and which no cold can chill ... This subterranean fire has its altar in each man's breast, for in the coldest day, and on the bleakest hill, the traveller cherishes a warmer fire within

the folds of his cloak than is kindled on any hearth. A healthy man, indeed, is the complement of the seasons, and in winter, summer is in his heart. There is the south.

The first energy you feel when walking is your own, that of your body in motion. It isn't an explosion of strength, but more a continuous and palpable radiance.

The Native Americans, whose wisdom Thoreau admired, regarded the Earth itself as a sacred source of energy. To stretch out on it brought repose, to sit on the ground ensured greater wisdom in councils, to walk in contact with its gravity gave strength and endurance. The Earth was an inexhaustible well of strength: because it was the original Mother, the feeder, but also because it enclosed in its bosom all the dead ancestors. It was the element in which transmission took place. Thus, instead of stretching their hands skyward to implore the mercy of celestial divinities, American Indians preferred to walk barefoot on the Earth:

> The Lakota was a true Naturist – a lover of Nature. He loved the earth and all things of the earth, the attachment growing with age. The old people came literally to love the soil and they sat or reclined on the ground with a feeling of being close to a mothering power. It was good for the skin to touch the earth and the old people liked to remove their moccasins and walk with bare feet on the sacred earth. Their tipis were built upon the earth and their altars were made of earth. The birds that flew in the air came to rest on the earth and it was the final abiding place of all things that lived and grew. The soil was soothing, strengthening, cleansing and healing. That is why the old Indian still sits upon the earth instead of propping

himself up and away from its life-giving forces. For him, to sit or lie upon the ground is to be able to think more deeply and to feel more keenly; he can see more clearly into the mysteries of life and come closer in kinship to other lives about him.

Walking, by virtue of having the earth's support, feeling its gravity, resting on it with every step, is very like a continuous breathing in of energy. But the earth's force is not transmitted only in the manner of a radiation climbing through the legs. It is also through the coincidence of circulations: walking is movement, the heart beats more strongly, with a more ample beat, the blood circulates faster and more powerfully than when the body is at rest. And the earth's rhythms draw that along, they echo and respond to each other.

A last source of energy, after the heart and the Earth, is landscapes. They summon the walker and *make him at home*: the hills, the colours, the trees all confirm it. The charm of a twisting path among hills, the beauty of vine fields in autumn, like purple and gold scarves, the silvery glitter of olive leaves against a defining summer sky, the immensity of perfectly sliced glaciers ... all these things support, transport and nourish us.

13

Pilgrimage

Walking isn't always an aimless stroll, a solitary wander. Historically it has sometimes taken codified forms which governed its conduct, termination and purpose. Pilgrimage is one of these major cultural forms.

The primary meaning of *peregrinus* is foreigner or exile. The pilgrim, originally, is not one who is heading somewhere (Rome, Jerusalem, etc.), but essentially one who *is not at home where he is walking*. In other words, not a stroller taking a few turns around the neighbourhood after dinner, or a landowner making a Sunday round of his plantations. For the pilgrim is never at home where he walks: he's a stranger, a foreigner. We are all, say the Church Fathers, fleetingly on this earth, passing through, and so we ought always to provide a night's shelter in our dwellings, to see our possessions as a disposable burden, and our friends as people met by the wayside.

A brief cascade of words, some remarks on the weather, a couple of handshakes, then goodbye: 'Fare well.' Every man is a pilgrim in this vale of tears, the Fathers say: his whole life is an exile, for his true dwelling-place can never be reached here below. And the whole Earth is a make-shift shelter. The Christian passes through this life like a walker in any country: without stopping. These lines, for example, are found in the chant of the Compostela pilgrim: 'Companion, we must make our way / Without lingering.'

Perhaps the itinerant monks called 'Gyrovagues' were especially responsible for promoting this view of our condition as eternal strangers. They journeyed ceaselessly from monastery to monastery, without fixed abode, and they haven't quite disappeared, even today: it seems there are still a handful tramping Mount Athos. They walk for their entire lives on narrow mountain paths, back and forth on a long repeated round, sleeping at nightfall wherever their feet have taken them; they spend their lives murmuring prayers on foot, walk all day without destination or goal, this way or that, taking branching paths at random, turning, returning, without going anywhere, illustrating through endless wandering their condition as permanent strangers in this profane world.

But the Gyrovagues were not much appreciated. These perpetual nomads were denigrated as profiteers and vagabonds, and the established Church condemned the itinerant mode of life. St Benedict in particular imposed 'monastic stability', asserting that the believer's condition of eternal pilgrimage (*peregrinatio perpetua*) was merely a metaphor, a metaphor that ought not to be squandered on the road, so much as deepened through the detachment of monastic prayer and contemplation. Several centuries earlier the Church Fathers, notably in Egypt, had already drawn a careful distinction between the pilgrim and the hermit. Of course *xenateia* (the condition of foreignness to the world) was to be exalted, but not manifested in suspect vagabondage; simple contemplative retreat would suffice.

Peregrinatio perpetua emphasizes the wish to leave, tear oneself away, renounce. Christ invited his disciples to take to the road: to leave their wives and children, their lands, their businesses and status, to go forth to spread the Word ('Sell all that you own, give it to the poor and follow me'). And much earlier still, the act of Abraham: leave everything ('Go into a place that I will show you ...'). You walk to have done with it all and purge yourself: to have done with the world's clamour, the accumulation of tasks, the wear and tear. And there's nothing better for forgetting, for not being *here* anymore, than the great boredom of the roads, the limitless monotony of forest paths. Walk, cut yourself off, depart, leave.

When you really walk, farewell follows farewell all day long. You can never be quite sure of ever setting foot in a place again. This condition of departure adds intensity to the gaze. That backward look when you cross a ridge, just before the landscape tilts. Or the final glance at last night's lodging as you leave in the morning (its grey mass, the trees behind). You turn round again, one more time ... but that restless gaze doesn't aim to grasp, possess or keep: rather it aims to give, to leave a little of its light in the stubborn presence of the rocks and flowers. The walker on nameless glaciers, under futureless skies, across plains devoid of history, scatters the flashes of his gaze into the very substance of things. When he walks, it is to cut through the world's opacity.

The pilgrim is not only a metaphor for the human condition. He also has a concrete, historical existence. Throughout the Middle Ages he was, we know, a distinct, differentiated character. A pilgrim had a specific juridical status. People adopted the condition of pilgrim officially, ritually, in public, with a solemn High Mass, after which the bishop blessed the walker's traditional kit: the staff (a long stick with a metal ferrule to help him walk, and fight off dogs or wild animals), a mendicant's pouch to hold the day's bread and essential documents. This bag had to be small (for survival was essentially ensured by faith in God), made of animal skin (a reminder of mortality), and always open, because a pilgrim is disposed to give, share, exchange. The pilgrim was also identified by his broad-brimmed hat (turned up at the front to display a scallop shell if he had been to Santiago de Compostela), short tunic and voluminous cloak.

On the occasion of his induction Mass, the bishop or parish priest would issue the pilgrim with a covering letter to serve as a safe-conduct during the journey, giving entry to monasteries and hospices that he would pass en route, and also (it was hoped) protecting him from highway robbers who might leave a consecrated walker alone for fear of punishment from on high. The ceremony was very solemn and grave, because this departure was like a small death. To reach Rome or Santiago, not to mention Jerusalem, would take months, with no guarantee of returning. You could die of exhaustion, be murdered by robbers, drown in a shipwreck or fall over a cliff. Hence the pilgrim, before leaving, had to make peace with his enemies, settle his outstanding disputes, and even make a will.

So why go at all, if the conditions were so difficult? The motives were numerous. In the first place, to augment devotion, to bear witness to one's faith. *Devotionis causa.* Because above and beyond the primary *peregrinatio* (the human condition of wandering through this vale of tears), each pilgrimage was assigned a specific goal, a final, radiant destination: visiting a sanctuary. Obviously the main sites of pilgrimage were the tombs of apostles or saints: St James in Compostela, St Paul and St Peter in Rome, Christ's empty sepulchre in Jerusalem; more modestly, St Martin's tomb at Tours, or the archangel Michael's relics at Mont-Saint-Michel. Pilgrimage testified to faith. It involved continuous asceticism in the humility of walking, accompanied by frequent fasts and constant prayer.

But a pilgrimage could also be undertaken as a penance for very serious faults. If a pious individual or a cleric confessed to a terrible sin weighing on his conscience – a huge blasphemy, or even a homicide that had escaped human justice – the penance could consist of a pilgrimage, its distance corresponding to the gravity of the offence. Some civil jurisdictions in the Middle Ages could impose a long pilgrimage for heavy crimes (such as parricide or rape), with the added advantage that it removed the offender. And in their time, the courts of the Inquisition sometimes imposed this temporary exile on heretics.

While the strain and suffering inherent to travel at that time made pilgrimage suitable as a mild punishment, it could be made less mild by specific conditions: walking barefoot, or hampered by being made to wear shackles on one's arms, legs or neck. The iron or steel bands – sometimes forged out of the weapon used to commit the crime – were apt to rust and break apart after months of fatigue and sweat.

Even without these terrible conditions, enduring long months of rain, cold and sunburn (for the pilgrim was totally *exposed*) could be a very gruelling experience. Then as now, the feet ended by becoming a constant fount of suffering: suppurating sores, painful gashes ... The ritual washing of a pilgrim's feet when he arrived at a monastery, apart from demonstrating the monks' Christ-like humility, reminds us that the pilgrim was a figure entitled to special consideration.

As well as demonstrating faith and expiating sins, pilgrimages were undertaken to ask for intercession. If a close relation or friend was sick, or if you yourself had a serious illness, you might seek the help of a saint by visiting their grave, on the assumption that a simple prayer wouldn't be as effective as a personal visit, when you can utter your prayer aloud within earshot of the tomb. But that in turn assumes a long walk to get there, so that one would approach the holy shrine purified by pain and effort. For fatigue purifies, destroys pride, and renders prayer more transparent.

And having arrived at the holy place, you would put in your prayer for intercession with the greatest humility, underlined by your battered feet and dusty apparel. If you yourself were the afflicted individual, you would try to touch the tomb, to cling to it as long as possible, with as much contact as you could manage between your ailing body and its surface, then lie down and spend a night nearby to ensure the best chance of absorbing regenerative strength from the healing relics within.

Finally, the faithful might use pilgrimage to give thanks to God for a specific favour – a saved life, a gift allowed, a restoration of health. Thus, Descartes, having been enlightened with his method, made a pilgrimage to the church of Notre-Dame-de-Lorette in Paris. Thousands of more modest believers, whose prayers seeking help for themselves or their families had been answered, took to the road and headed for the nearest holy place to show their gratitude.

We should try, however, to tone down some of the archetypal imagery. The pilgrim is often represented in legendary style as a lone walker, staff in hand, dressed in a simple homespun robe, striding through sheets of rain, thunder muttering in the distance. As night descends, he knocks on the immense door of a towering stone monastery, illuminated by flashes of lightning. In reality, pilgrimages were usually made in small groups, for reasons of security, and often on horseback, especially when the distances were great.

But that did not exempt anyone from setting their feet on the ground as soon as the destination became visible, when they could see the church spire or cathedral tower in the distance. It was necessary to arrive on foot, an obligation that combined several lessons. The first was a reminder of Christ's poverty and humility, the walker being poor among the poor. The only wealth of a poor man is his body. The walker is a son of the soil. Every step is an acceptance of gravity, every step underlines the connection and beats on the earth as a promised, final grave. But walking was also arduous, demanding sustained effort. One could only make a proper approach to a holy shrine after being purified by suffering, and walking required an endlessly repeated effort.

~

The first main routes for Christians led to Rome or Jerusalem. From the third century, Jerusalem became the ultimate pilgrimage for Christians, an immersion in the presence of Christ: treading the very soil on which he had walked (in loco ubi steterunt pedes eius, in the words of the Psalm), following the path of Calvary, touching the wood from the True Cross, gazing into the cave where he had spoken to his disciples. But widespread social and political unrest made the journey increasingly difficult, and soon Rome became a safer, more reliable destination.

The resting place of the leading apostles, Peter and Paul, Rome was the hub and centre of the established Catholic Church. Thus to perform the *peregrinatio romana* was a perfect act of submission, expressing profound loyalty to the Church in fulfilment of its historic mission. Then, after 1300, great jubilee years were decreed, during which going to Rome and following a specific route inside that city from sanctuary to sanctuary (St Peter's, St John Lateran, St Paul Outside the Walls ...) would earn a full remission of all the pilgrim's sins. Rome was a place to testify, but also to seek salvation.

Compostela was the last of these major destinations. It is said of St James – one of Christ's three favourites, and the first martyred apostle, decapitated by order of King Herod – that his own disciples loaded his remains onto a ship which was then wrecked on the shores of Galicia. The heavy marble casket was carried ashore, and there forgotten – until the famous moment when a hermit called Pelagius dreamed that angels had shown him the exact location of the tomb, whose direction was being indicated every night by a row of stars. A sanctuary was built over the rediscovered sepulchre, then a church, and finally a cathedral. Santiago de Compostela became one of the most famous sites of pilgrimage, soon taking its place beside Rome and Jerusalem.

The explanation for the very rapid development of this destination, after its late start, has much to do with reasons of convenience. Of course it is the tomb of a major saint, but one that was perhaps easier to reach (lower passes, more peaceable regions) than those of Peter and Paul – although the distance from northern Europe was much the same – and in any case nearer than Jerusalem.

Rome and Jerusalem are both cities of such mystical intensity that the road to get there can only be a long succession of uninteresting landmarks and mediations. The radiance of the place itself shrivels the singularity of the stages leading up to it. Especially when, there at last, a new progression is required. In Rome, the itinerary goes from the basilica of St Peter via St John Lateran and St Paul Outside the Walls to St Mary Major; from the Holy Cross of Jerusalem to St Lawrence Outside the Walls. There was a visit to the catacombs, long subterranean corridors lined with the coffins of early martyrs. So, after an unending linear road, the real path of devotion is paced out in the Eternal City.

Jerusalem is something else again: Christians must complete the Stations of the Cross. After gathering in the sanctuary of the Holy Sepulchre, they follow the Via Dolorosa; they climb, in the east of the city, the Mount of Olives where the Agony occurred; they walk in the Garden of Gethsemane, the scene of Christ's last night, and reach the chamber where the Last Supper took place, behind the ramparts on the Hill of Zion, at whose foot a church marks the spot where Peter denied Christ three times. And beyond that, one can push on to Bethlehem, two hours' walk, and further still, well to the north, reach the banks of Lake Tiberias, where Christ played as a child; and seek in Nazareth the Grotto of the Annunciation. Thus in Jerusalem as in Rome, the authentic pilgrimage only starts when you arrive.

At Santiago there is just one cathedral, shining in solitary splendour, unique as the sun and the end of the road. It can be spied from the last cairn, eliciting cries of happiness from the weary pilgrim of yore, who immediately set foot on the ground if mounted, and took off his shoes if on foot, because he had to arrive in a posture of humility. Arriving at Santiago really is arriving *at the end*. And might not its geographical position have contributed to the magic of Compostela? Situated at Europe's westernmost point (walking, Thoreau wrote, means going West), at the world's end (*finis terrae*: beyond it extends an ocean that for aeons appeared definitive). To go towards Santiago one had to move steadily along with the sun.

People don't talk about the road to Rome or to Jerusalem in the same way that they speak of the roads to Santiago. The mystical intensity of the tomb is not so powerful, so glaring that it overshadows the long trek to reach it. On the contrary, it illuminates the journey. Compostela completes it, but does not cancel it out. The success of Santiago owed as much to the journey as to the final destination. The mystical grandeur of the Galician pilgrimage resides in the sacralization of the route along with the sanctuary. The route, or rather the *routes*. What road should one take, which adventure?

The great invention of Compostela was the establishment of defined roads, with defined stages, and obligatory visits en route: four main routes, with innumerable secondary variations. When you started from Vézelay, after gathering at the shrine of Mary Magdalene – after shedding tears for the one who bathed Christ's feet in her own tears – you went on to Noblat, to the sepulchre of St Leonard, 'deliverer of those who sit in darkness'; leaving from Tours, where the body of St Martin lies, you stopped at Angély where rests the venerable head (*venerandum caput*) of St John the Baptist, then at Saintes where you could gather near the body of St Eutropius, put to death by 150 butchers; from Sainte-Marie-du-Puy (the Via Podiensis), you went to venerate the body of St Faith, virgin and martyr, at Conques; starting from the tomb of St Giles, you would visit the body of St Sernin in Toulouse …

Thus the 'Guide for the Pilgrim to Compostela', a thirteenth-century text included in the Codex Calixtinus, sets out various itineraries leading from one saint's body to another, all thaumaturges, healers; from tomb to tomb, every one enclosing the author of spectacular miracles. And that repetition of holy presence was architecturally underlined by the resemblance between the great churches on the way, sisters on the road to Compostela. Roads therefore supplied with many sanctuaries all alike, but also with monasteries to give pilgrims a night's shelter, and hospices to care for those exhausted, and sometimes give them the last rites; but roads too that were perhaps so many chapters of a great book.

Joseph Bédier, a historian of mediaeval literature, wrote: 'In the beginning was the road …' The beginning, he meant, of the narrative, the novel, the epic poem. At the beginning of our literature, we would have found pilgrims' roads. Bédier's view is that early epic poems were born there, in the dust of the roads to Compostela. The pilgrimage was long. People stopped for the night, talked until late, reciting an epic version heard elsewhere on some other night. They mixed in other episodes, juxtaposed sequences, until in the end a single vast poem had been assembled, which would then be fixed in writing. That is the true miracle of Compostela: to have completed the miracle of the major saint (*primus ex apostolis*, says the marching canticle) with the miracle of the road.

14

Regeneration and Presence

Behind every pilgrimage we find a utopia and a myth: the myth of regeneration and the utopia of presence. I like to think that St James embodies the virtues of pilgrimage so well because he is identified as the first witness to the Transfiguration of Christ. Internal transformation remains the pilgrim's mystical ideal: he hopes to be absolutely *altered* on his return. That transformation is still expressed in the vocabulary of regeneration: very often there is a spring, stream or river close to holy places, the lustral element in which pilgrims can immerse themselves, to emerge purified, as it were cleansed of themselves. A well-known instance is the annual Hindu festival in the upper Ganges.

As an example of this utopia of rebirth through walking, I would cite the pilgrimage to Mount Kailash in Tibet, a splendidly solitary mountain, a dome of ice sitting on an immense plateau, and regarded by many Oriental religions as a holy place: the centre of the universe. Pilgrims depart from the great plains of India. There follows a journey of several hundred kilometres across the Himalayan ranges, freezing passes alternating with deep, stifling valleys. The road is exhausting and includes all the trials and risks of mountain country: steep paths, vertical cliffs. Little by little you lose your identity and memories along the way, until you are nothing but an endlessly walking body.

Crossing a pass, one arrives at last in the Puyrang valley. Suddenly you are in a different landscape, a shining, transparent minerality. No more heaped dark rocks topped with snowy peaks, no more forests of black pines wreathed in whitish fogs. Nothing but the simple and pure contrast of earth and sky. A landscape from the world's beginnings, a desert of grey, green and buff. The pilgrim, emptied of his past, trudging through that arid transparency, can already see in the distance another range of mountains, symmetrical and glittering. Then he is truly nothing, and the slow winding between black lakes and gilded hillsides over a leaden earth is his Lesson in the Shades.

There is another pass to be crossed before he reaches the Land of the Gods. Courage is given by the fabulous sight of a white dome coming into view, set like a reclining icy sun, motionless: the summit of Kailash, guiding and summoning the traveller. At last he crosses the Gula

Pass, more than 5,000 metres high, and there the impression is shattering, like a lasting bolt of lightning that works into the soul: sudden, definitive immensity. Below extends a lake, deep blue in colour (Manasarovar). And Mount Kailash is at last fully visible in its enormous, motionless completeness.

The air is so pure and clear that every shape glitters. There lies the sacred mountain, facing the walker: navel of the earth, axis of the universe, absolute centre. And the pilgrim, in the vertigo induced by this vision, is simultaneously victor and vanquished. Every truly magnificent landscape diminishes the person who has conquered it on foot, and at the same time fills him with victorious energy. Two impulses run through him at once: to give a shout of triumph and to collapse in tears. He dominates the mountain with his gaze, but is crushed by the vision at the same time. The incredible vibration that shakes the walker stems from this contradictory double impulse.

But also, for the Kailash pilgrim, the depersonalization pursued for months has given place to a void which is suddenly filled: there it is, right there, just here, in front of him! And the feeling is deepened by the presence of thousands of little cairns (three, four or five stones in a small pyramid) all around him, testimony to the thousands of pilgrims who, like him, have known exhaustion and ecstasy. The effect of presence given off by these innumerable stone offerings, like everlasting flowers on the ground, is enormous: each seems to beckon, producing a sort of shimmer, as if one were surrounded by ghosts.

There still remains the circuit of the sacred mountain, which takes several days: Oriental ritual tends to impose a prayerful circuit on foot of the holy place (circumambulation), and Mount Kailash is like a natural temple, a sacred monument sculpted in ice by the gods. And above all, the ultimate test awaits the pilgrim: the Dolma La Pass, altitude 5,800 metres, before he can descend once more into the valleys. And on reaching those hostile, frozen heights, the pilgrim stops, stretches out on the stones like a dying man, and thinks of all those he has failed to love, praying for them, reconciling himself to his past before leaving it for good. Then he descends to the Lake of Compassion (the emerald-coloured Gauri Kund) to wash away his identity, his history. There the cycle ends. The pilgrim however is reborn not to himself, but to detachment, indifference to physical contingencies, universal benevolence.

Pilgrimage can also carry a utopia of *cosmic* rebirth. A good example is the great peyote walk accomplished annually by the Huichol people of Mexico. This community, which lives in a remote region of the high Sierra Madre, every year (starting in October, after the maize harvest), in small groups, covers more than 400 kilometres of stony tracks and dusty roads to the Potosí desert; there the peyote grows, a small spineless cactus that combines medicinal virtues with hallucinogenic powers. They collect the peyote buttons in big wicker baskets and return home, singing.

The long walk is preceded by elaborate preparations in the home village, sacrifices and rituals including a deer hunt, the animal's blood anointing the offerings for the great gods who will be encountered on the way. Each participant will bear a ritual name during the journey, will have a strictly determined place in the order of procession, will personify a god or a function, will be compelled to undergo major fasts, drinking only at fixed times, accepting rigid sexual abstinence, and on the fifth day of the journey will submit to a complete public confession. The object of the pilgrimage is to reach Wirikuta, the Land of the Ancestors where the peyote grows.

The stages are always the same, fixed by tradition back in the mists of time. During the journey, the shaman who guides them – he knows all the narratives and all the formulae of protection and salvation – reads the landscape being crossed like the pages of a great book. At a bend in the path, he stops, utters a humble request, then opens the empty space by sweeping it ceremonially with the feathers on his sacred staff: only then can he pass the 'Door to the Clouds'. Each door gives access to a new sacred space. All along the road, the topography of the surface, the placement of trees, the disposition of rocks, have a history: here the stones scattered on the ground are a sheaf of arrows forgotten by an absent-minded Ancestor; there, a cluster of marshes represents the source of all the world's springs (this muddy pool is none other than a footprint left by a god, from which a spring gushes). The stops are lengthy, with ritual ablutions, placement of offerings, feathered darts planted in the banks. Then the journey resumes, eventually reaching the mountain of the sun, in a totally arid landscape.

Under the mountain lies the Land of the Ancestors. The pilgrims' faces go blank: the place is saturated with myths, with sacred presences. Suddenly the expedition leader says he sees a large stag. The recall is total. They follow the chief. In the place of the apparition, he sends the point of an arrow into the ground: the horns of the invisible stag are brought low; in their place appears a big cactus. In this way the story of the god is retold, for peyote was born when the Sun god launched an arrow of light at the Stag god whose horns, falling to the ground, were transformed into the precious cactus.

Around the peyote plant, with many invocations, a multitude of offerings are made, and it is called upon to give the pilgrims its power and magic. Only then does the shaman uproot the peyote; he gives a piece to each pilgrim who eats it, intoning as he does so: 'You who have come seeking life: here is life!' The pilgrims will spend three days at Wirikuta, gathering the holy plant, filling their wicker baskets, consuming a little every evening and staying awake late (each man's dreams are carefully analysed and will help determine social life and organization in the coming year). Then they will retrace the 400 kilometres of road to their homes.

The Huichol accomplish this annual journey not only to harvest a cactus that serves the group as a universal remedy, a stimulant, but also to *keep the world going*. Peyote represents the god of Fire who forms, with Maize and the Stag, a sacred trinity. The mythology has it that the first expedition was organized by a primitive god (the one who triumphed over the shades and death) to impose the alternation of dry and

rainy seasons, a balance between the powers of Fire and
Water. It is on this division that life depends: maize needs
water and sunshine. And repeating that founding expedition is a way to ensure cosmic balance, guarantee the
stability of the universe. You have to walk to *keep the world
going*. A myth of rebirth, then, both personal and cosmic.

Pilgrimage also gives access to a utopia of presence. We
have mentioned the importance of reliquaries as favoured
pilgrimage destinations. On entering the sanctuary, the
pilgrim is directly *present*: present to the saint's body which
is really there, under its cloak of marble, radiating its force
so that the stone is charged with it; present on the hill
where the Saviour's shadow once fell, and where it persists
as an eternal echo. No question of being a symbol, an image
or interpretation: it is really *there*. But to get there you must
walk: walking in itself, as it takes time, establishes presence.
When you reach the foot of a mountain, having approached
it from afar, it isn't just the eye that perceives an image: the
body, in its muscles and sinews, has been feeding on it at
length. The image itself is simply an introduction. If I get
out of a car to face a monument, a church or temple, I see
them, I scrutinize them, but they are just images. I appre-
hend them quickly, a specific photograph, the image of an
image. Presence is something that takes time: you have to
glimpse from a distance, from the last hill of Avallon, the
sudden appearance of Vézelay Abbey, and then approach
slowly, see how the slowly fading light transforms it, you
have to lose sight of it and find it again, guess where it is ...
But as we walk on we know it hasn't moved, and is drawing

us. When the pilgrim at last sets down his bundle, and can *stop* because he has done it, he's *arrived*, he hardly needs to feast his eyes on the conquered vision: his body is filled with it from head to toe.

Then the entire day is transfigured. To arrive on foot at a place whose name one has dreamed of all day, whose picture has lain for so long in the mind, casts a backward light over the road. And what was accomplished in fatigue, sometimes boredom, in the face of that absolutely solid presence that justifies it all, is transformed into a series of necessary and joyous moments. Walking makes time reversible.

15

The Cynic's Approach

Was the Greek sage a good walker? Legend would have it so, for he is usually depicted standing, strolling among his disciples, walking up and down a length of colonnade or a grove of trees, pausing from time to time, turning round, moving off in another direction, always followed by jostling pupils. Thus Raphael, in his famous painting *The School of Athens*, drew the prototype of philosophers in Antiquity: upright, the tread firm, the index finger authoritative.

Socrates, as we know, could not keep still. He was always taking a stroll in the agora, especially on market days when it was crowded. And he could be heard from a distance asking endless questions. But it wasn't walking that he liked, it was finding people to talk to in public squares or outside stadiums. Xenophon in his *Memorabilia* wrote that 'He was always visible. For in the early morning he used to go on walks and to the gymnasia, and when the agora was full he was visible there, and for the remainder of the day he was always where he might be with the most people' (I, 1, 10). But for all that, Socrates was not a great walker. In Plato's *Phaedrus* he is seen as indifferent to walking, resistant to the countryside: Nature had not enough to say to him (230d).

In a somewhat elliptical reference, Diogenes Laertius suggests that Plato could have taught while walking about (III, 27). Aristotle himself probably owed his nickname 'Walker' (*peripatêtikos*, V, 2) to the same practice. Unless he was so called after the place where he taught: for he established his school (the Lyceum) by taking over a former gymnasium on the banks of the Ilissos, which included a peristyle (*peripatos*). *Peripatein* is a Greek verb meaning 'to walk', but it also has the meaning 'to converse', 'to engage in dialogue while walking'. Diogenes Laertius says of Aristotle that he had skinny legs, and once he had a good number of disciples he preferred to sit.

The Stoics had already abandoned teaching on the hoof, but – as in the school of Epictetus – the master challenged an audience that should be imagined standing still. As for the Epicureans, who disliked fuss and movement, we should think of them hidden among gardens, conversing calmly in the shade of big trees.

The only Greek sages who were authentic walkers were

the Cynics,* forever on the move, shuffling like vagabonds about the streets. Like dogs. Always rambling from city to city, from public square to public square.

It was from their demeanour and physical appearance that they were recognized. In one hand they carried a stout staff, on their shoulders a piece of thick fabric that served as blanket, overcoat and roof, and at their side a mendicant's bag containing 'three times nothing'. They had done so much walking that they hardly needed shoes or even sandals, the soles of their feet being much like leather. The mediaeval pilgrim resembled them; even more so the preachers of mendicant orders. They did their walking not so much to teach as to provoke and upset. They practised the art of diatribe rather than of predication. They insulted and shocked people with their verbal attacks.

Apart from their appearance, their language was the thing that identified them. In fact they hardly spoke, but rather barked, a raucous, aggressive discourse. When they reached their destination in the public square, after walking for days, people flocked to hear them bawling, haranguing the rapt mass of the crowd, all hugely enjoying the furious rant, but vaguely disturbed by it too. For everyone felt accused and criticized for their habits, conduct and convictions. These sermons were not, however, erudite demonstrations

---

* The term 'cynic' is derived from the Greek noun kunos, meaning dog. It designated a character whose mode of behaviour was very rough, who spent his time haranguing the crowd and denouncing the world's hypocrisies. This is remote from the modern sense of 'cynicism', which signifies an attempt to extract the maximum profit from a system without regard for the most elementary human values.

or moral dissertations. The Cynic barked, in short angry yaps, but insistently. Rather, a series of summonses, quips that cut in all directions, white-hot imprecations that spread like dye.

All the commonplace compromises and conventions were booed, mocked, dragged through the mud: marriage, respect for hierarchies, cupidity, egotism, the quest for recognition, cowardice, vice, rapacity. Nothing was spared, everything was denounced, accused, ridiculed, from the nomad perspective.

The Cynics' philosophy is linked with the condition of the walker by far more than the superficial impression of rootlessness: the dimensions of experience inherent in those great peregrinations become dynamite when imported into towns.

~

The Cynic's coarse, boorish lifestyle featured a primary experience of the elemental. Remember that he was confronted by the elements in all their power and even brutality – freezing wind, lashing rain, burning sun. He was exposed to them by walking, and by his destitution, devoid of a dwelling place and possessions alike. But by the same token he could rediscover a *truth* in that primitive condition. The elemental is the truth of what holds fast, resists, is unmoved by passing circumstance. Elemental truth is wild, and shares in the energy of the elements.

Philosophers of the type one might call sedentary enjoy

contrasting the appearance with the essence of things. Behind the curtain of tangible sights, behind the veil of visibilities, they try to identify what is pure and essential, hoping perhaps to display, above the colours of the world, the glittering, timeless transparency of their own thought. The palpable is a lie, a shifting scatter of appearances, the body is a screen, and the real truth is assembled in the soul, in thought, in the mind.

The Cynic cut through that classic opposition. He was not out to seek or reconstruct some truth behind appearances. He would flush it out from the radical nature of immanence: just below the world's images, he was hunting for what supported them. The elemental: nothing true but sun, wind, earth and sky, their truth residing in their unsurpassable vigour. For the tangible, avoided by the deskbound philosopher aiming to find refuge in eternal intelligibility, was still too complex and diverse. It was a mishmash of everything: houses, forests, monuments, precipices. There was no hurry to go beyond appearances. The authentic ascetic should plunge into things, dig into the tangible to find the absolutely elemental as energy, until resistance is felt.

But the reason this discovery energizes the Cynic (who is not a hermit living solely on the breath of Being) is that it is political: it should serve to shatter the derisory grand postures of the stoop-shouldered philosopher, hunched over his internal wealth; to burst open the poverty of his hidden essential truths, expose the superficiality of his lectures and books. Truth is the elements taken in all their savage vigour; the wind that buffets the skin, the dazzling sun, the

storms of thunder and lightning. To experience those is also
to grasp a primitive energy that makes a mockery of the sage
and his solemn rictuses.

~

The second experience raised by the nomad condition is
that of the *raw*. Writers of the time often mentioned the
scandalous behaviour of the Cynics in devouring raw meat.
Is not Diogenes said to have died from trying to eat a live
octopus? It wasn't only their diet that was raw, but their
language and manners too.

That rawness, that rusticity in their behaviour and condition, is again a battering ram against another great classical
opposition. The sedentary philosopher liked to distinguish
between the natural and the artificial. What the Cynics
called Nature was the marshalling of each thing to its
essence, each being coinciding with its definition. And that
transparent identity with the self can be shuffled through
artifice: the artifice of discourse, of social arrangements, of
political laws. So it's necessary to find each time, just behind
what is presented, the calm truth of each thing.

Just as the Cynic had released the essence of the elemental, so he had subverted the natural. Nature to him was
rawness. The raw was Nature on the level of elemental need.
Nature, but not the dreamy utopian Nature of a sojourn
among quiet truths. The raw is uncivilized Nature, wild
and tempestuous, Nature impolite, scandalous, shame-
less, inhuman. The body functions without reference to

conventions or rules. Nudity is raw; defecation and mastur-
bation are raw. Eating is a matter for the stomach, nothing
more, to fill and empty it. The dog has no manners when he
sleeps or satisfies his needs: he just does it. When Diogenes,
hanging about near a banquet one day, started imprecat-
ing loudly against the idiocy of the gathering, someone
tossed him a bone still covered with meat, contemptu-
ously as if feeding a dog. Diogenes seized the bone and
gnawed it greedily, then climbed onto the table and pissed
over the revellers. 'I eat like you, gentlemen, and I piss
like you'.

The Cynic was not immoral. But he used the simple
assertion of his body, on the level of its biological functions,
to denounce and expose men's tawdry good education,
received values and hypocrisies when they speak of Nature.
The fact is that it had become, via those sedentary sages, a
sort of diplomatic bag for social conventions and cultural
moulds: everything had gone through on the quiet. The
raw was revolutionary.

~

Thirdly, the Cynic lived, obviously, out of doors. So then
sometimes, of course, a providential barrel was put to use;
but in the end he had no home. He slept in ditches, or
against walls, wrapped in his cloak. He was permanently
exposed not only (as we have seen) to the great forces of
nature, but to the public gaze. He ate in public, frolicked
amorously too in the open air, as Crates and Hipparchia did.

The 'outside' espoused by the Cynics destabilized the traditional contrast between public and private. The distinction was of interest only to the sedentary: a choice between two closed circles, both shielded from the great outdoors. Private meant the intimacy of family passions, the secrets of desire, the protection of walls, property. Public meant ambition and reputation, the scramble for recognition, the regard of others, social identities.

But the Cynic was *outside*. And it was from that elsewhere, that exteriority to the world of men, that he could equate low private acts and public vices. It was from that outside that he barracked, mocked and threw together the private and the public as a brace of petty human expedients.

~

A final dimension of the travelling Cynic's life was necessity. The necessary isn't imposed, like something inevitable; it is discovered, it unveils itself, it is conquered. Here again, a traditional system of oppositions is subverted: the contrast of useful and futile. The philosopher bent over his desk thinks he has reflected a great deal, when he deems that a bed is useful, but that it is futile to require a canopied bed if all one wants is to sleep; or that it is useful to drink from a glass, but that it doesn't take a gold goblet to refresh oneself. These were vain distinctions to the Cynics, because they fell short of the test of the necessary.

At the fountain one day Diogenes saw a child drinking from the joined palms of his hands. The Cynic stopped short, thunderstruck, and declared: 'Diogenes, you have been outdone!' Then he took a wooden goblet from his meagre bundle and flung it far from him with a smile of triumph. Happy, because he had found another way to disencumber himself.

That is the necessary: an ascetic's conquest. It is not a question of saying, like the desk-bound philosophers, that you have to be able to detach yourself from all the useless possessions that burden us, but of digging a little deeper, past the useful, down to the necessary. It's more than frugality: being content with little, being careful. The task here is more arduous, difficult, demanding: to accept only the necessary. This transition takes us well beyond resignation, and leads to the assertion of an absolute sovereignty. For the necessary, conquered beyond the useful, overturns the meaning of destitution.

~

The walker is king, and the earth is his domain. The necessary, once conquered, is never lacking, for it is everywhere and belongs to all, the property of none. Whence comes this final reversal, from poverty to wealth.

After all – as the Epicureans had shown – he is rich who lacks for nothing. And the Cynic lacked for nothing, because he had discovered the pleasures of the necessary: the ground to rest his body, what he found to eat during his wanderings, the starry sky for a ceiling, springs to drink from. Well beyond the useful and the futile, the necessary suddenly made the entire world of cultural objects appear trivial, alienating, cumbersome, *impoverishing*.

I am richer (the Cynic said) than any great landowner, for the earth is my domain. My properties are unbounded. My house is bigger than any other, or rather I have as many as I want: hollows among the rocks, caves in the hills. I have in store more food and drink than any man, I gorge on spring water.

Nor did the Cynic recognize frontiers, being at home wherever he could walk. A citizen of the world, not because, having nothing left to lose, he could finally imagine gaining everything, but because the elemental quality, the bare necessities, and the rawness of the world are there in limitless profusion. His was not a projected, ideal, future cosmopolitanism, a regulatory idea, a fictional world or promise. It was achieved absolutely in his rootlessness. The Cynic held to nothing, was attached to nothing. Absolutely free, he displayed his provoking health, his unlimited and endlessly shareable sovereignty. Who are you, he said, to be giving lessons? I am a citizen of the world, and it is from that outside that I address you. Epictetus makes him proclaim:

Behold me! I have neither city nor house nor possessions nor servants: the ground is my couch; I have no wife, no children, no shelter – nothing but earth and sky, and one poor cloak. And what lack I yet? Am I not untouched by sorrow, by fear? Am I not free?

16

States of Well-Being

Everything is valued the same nowadays: joy, pleasure, serenity, happiness ... In their day, the sages of Antiquity took care to draw distinctions between these states of well-being. Such separations had particular importance, since it was through them that the schools of philosophy distinguished themselves from one another. For while all agreed that wisdom should enable people to approach a full flowering of their being, the sects based their divergences on the definition of that plenitude – the purpose of life, and the object of immense study. Cyrenaics, Epicureans, Sceptics, Platonists, each school's sages presented an absolutely distinct state of fulfilment, based on joy, happiness or serenity.

There was nothing sectarian about the walking experience, however. In a precise manner, it was open to all these possibilities, offering the chance to experience all these states, to different degrees, on different occasions. It was a practical introduction to all the great ancient wisdoms.

Pleasure first, perhaps. Pleasure is a matter of encountering. It is a possibility of feeling that finds completion in an encounter with a body, element or substance. That is all there is to pleasure: agreeable sensations, sweet, unprecedented, deliciously unexpected, wild ... It is always some sensation, and always triggered by an encounter, by something that confirms, from outside, the possibilities inscribed in our bodies. Pleasure is the encounter with the good object: the one that causes a possibility of feeling to blossom.

The accursed peculiarity of pleasure, very often discussed, is that repetition reduces its intensity. The good object that has fulfilled me can be consumed with renewed pleasure a second time, perhaps even more intensely because, being prepared, I adopt a posture of *appreciation*: I try to explore every dimension, to taste it in all its fullness. A third time, a fourth ... by now the furrows, the ruts, are already traced, and it becomes something known, or recognized. It's the same thing, the same fruit, the same wine, the same touch, but it is already traced faintly in my body: it no longer runs through it leaving a glowing mark. Because that intensity is what people seek in pleasure: that moment in which the faculties of feeling are overwhelmed, awakened, shaken up and challenged. It becomes flat with repetition, warmed over, tiresome, always the same. Hence a dual strategy: diversity or quantity. Either you change types, find other varieties, move on to different genres, or else you increase the dose. Both strategies work, a little, the first few times they are tried: some of the lost intensity is recovered. But the effects are too much anticipated, hoped for, tracked: there is an expectation of pleasure so exact that the pleasure is killed.

In walking, you find these moments of pure pleasure, around encounters. The scent of blackberries or myrtle, the gentle warmth of an early summer sun, the freshness of a stream. Something never known before. In this way walking permits, in bright bursts, that clearance of a path to feeling, in discreet quantities: a handful of encounters along the way.

~

Joy is another thing, less passive and more demanding, less intense and more complete, less local and richer. Joy too is experienced in walking, understood this time as the affect linked to an activity. The same fundamental idea can be found in Aristotle and Spinoza: joy is the accompaniment to an affirmation.

Sadness is passivity: when I just can't do it. I drive myself, I am constrained, everything resists. I endure, I try force. I start again and it's the same inertia: I don't get there. I dry up, staring at the blank page: too difficult. The words don't come, they drag their feet and butt each other like clumsy and grotesque pachyderms, lining up in wheezy disorder to form rickety sentences. Failure in sporting competition: too hard, legs like gateposts, body an anvil. It won't do what it's told and runs aground, a shapeless mass. Discouragement with a musical instrument: the fingers don't respond, they are like over-heavy mallets. The voice slips and changes register. The vocal cords creak. Or lastly, lassitude at work: too repetitive, too voluminous. Push the machine to keep going against boredom and fatigue. Nothing does the trick: sadness. Sadness is a blocked affirmation, hampered, contradicted, gone bad.

When I have to perform a difficult action, I start again, I persist, and then eventually the action works. After that I accomplish it easily, with increasing agility. Everything goes well and quickly. It's the same when training has overcome initial stiffness: the body lightens up, it *responds*. Joy is not the satisfied contemplation of an accomplished result, the emotion of victory, the satisfaction of having succeeded. It is the sign of an energy that is deftly deployed, it is a free affirmation: everything comes easy. Joy is an activity: executing with ease something difficult that has taken time to master, asserting the faculties of the mind and the body. Joys of thought when it finds and discovers, joys of the body when it achieves without effort. That is why joy, unlike pleasure, increases with repetition, and is enriched.

When you are walking, joy is a basso continuo. Locally, of course, you may run into effort and difficulty. You will also find immediate moments of contentment: a proud gaze backwards to contemplate the long steep plunge of the slope behind you. Those satisfactions, though, too often present an opportunity to reintroduce quantities, scores, figures (which track? how long? what altitude?). And walking becomes a competition. That is why expeditions in high mountain country (conquering peaks, each one a challenge) are always slightly impure: because they give rise to narcissistic gratification. What dominates in walking, away from ostentation and showing off, is the simple joy of feeling your body in the most primitively natural activity. Watch a small child taking his first steps, the radiance that comes over him in making one step after another. When you walk, the basso continuo of joy comes from feeling the extent to which the body is made for this movement, the way it finds in each pace the resource for the next.

Even apart from the action of walking, but compatible with it, there is also joy experienced as fullness, the joy of living. After a whole day's walking, the simple relaxation of taking the weight off your legs, satisfying your hunger simply, having a quiet drink and contemplating the declining daylight, the gentle fall of night.* The body free from hunger and thirst, without aches, the body at rest, the simple feeling of being alive is enough to produce the highest sort of joy, of pure intensity and absolute modesty: the joy of living, of feeling oneself here, tasting one's own presence in harmony with the world's. Alas, though, too many of us, for too long, have been ensnared by bad images into believing that plenitude depends on the possession of

---

* As fully described in Rimbaud's poem 'At the Green Inn' ('Blissfully happy, I stuck out my legs under the green table ...').

objects, on social prestige. We are already beyond that, we always have been. The experience of walking surely constitutes a reconquest of that state, because subjecting the body to a prolonged activity – which as we know brings joy, but also fatigue and boredom – causes the appearance, when it is at rest, of fullness or plenitude, that secondary, deeper, more fundamental joy, linked with a more secret affirmation: the body breathes gently, I am alive and I am here.

~

Also experienced while walking is what might be called 'happiness', often better described by writers and poets than great thinkers, since it is a matter of encounters and depends on situations. The *pleasure* that is taken in savouring wild berries from the hedgerow or the caress of a breeze on the cheeks; the *joy* of walking and feeling the body advancing 'like a man alone'; the *fullness* of feeling alive. And then *happiness*, before the spectacle of a violet-shadowed valley below the beams of the setting sun, that miracle of summer evenings, when for a few minutes every shade of colour, flattened all day by a steely sun, is brought out at last by the golden light, and breathes. Happiness can come later, at the guesthouse, in the company of others staying there: people met there, happy to find themselves together for a moment through chance. But all of that involves receiving.

Happiness involves finding oneself the recipient of a spectacle, a moment, an atmosphere, and taking, accepting and grasping the blessing of the moment. For that there can be no recipe, no preparation; one has to be there when the moment comes. Otherwise, it's something else: satisfaction in having achieved something, joy in doing what you know how to do. Happiness is fragile precisely because it is not repeatable; opportunities for it are rare and random, like gold threads in the world's fabric. They ought to be seized.

~

Lastly, the state of *serenity*, again something different: more than detachment, less than wonder; more than resignation, less than affirmation. A steady balance in the soul. Walking leads to it, quietly, gradually, through the very alternation of rest and movement. It is linked obviously with the slowness of walking, its absolutely repetitive character; you have to *bring yourself* to it.

Serenity means no longer being trapped in the agitated oscillations of fear and hope, and even placing yourself beyond all certainty (because certainties are defended, argued, constructed). When you have set off for the day, and know that it will take so many hours to reach the next stage, there's nothing left to do but walk, and follow the road. *Nothing else to do.* At all events, it will be long, every stride stepping over the seconds without shortening the hours. At all events, evening will come and the legs will have ended by engulfing, in small bites, the impossible distance. It is an inevitability with inevitable effects. There is virtually no need to decide, consider, calculate. Nothing to do but walk. You could think ahead perhaps, but at walking pace things

145

go too slowly for that. Anticipation would be discouraging. So you should just keep going, at your own pace, to the end of this leg of the journey.

Serenity comes from simply following the path. And then, while walking, serenity comes because all the hassles and dramas, all the things that gouge empty furrows in our lives and our bodies, becomes as if absolutely suspended, because out of range, too remote and incalculable. The wearisome grand passions and distasteful excitements of active lives, stressed to breaking point, are supplanted in the end by the implacable lassitude of walking: just walking. Serenity is the immense sweetness of no longer expecting anything, just walking, just moving on.

17

Melancholy Wandering – Nerval

Those is a lot of walking in Gérard de Nerval. People
tramping along, remembering, imagining, singing
a 'traditional song of the region' as they go:

> Courage, my friend, courage!
> We've almost reached the village!
> At the very first house we meet,
> We'll stop for something to eat!

Between long sessions in libraries – busy finding rare
manuscripts, tracing improbable genealogies and filling
in historical lacunae – and long hours of writing ('those
undoable books' as Dumas called them) or simple copying,
between visits to his few friends and evenings at the theatre

lusting after The One (the actress Jenny C. for whom he had an unrequited passion), there was time for walks and wanders.

I don't want to mention here the journeys in Germany, England, Italy, Holland or further afield in the Middle East (Alexandria, Cairo, Beirut, Constantinople), but rather those walks through the streets of Paris, when he would come down from Montmartre and lose himself in the alleys around Les Halles; or again those long promenades in the forests at Ermenonville or Mortefontaine, in the woods at Pont-Armé, Saint-Laurent, or again the banks of the Aisne or the Thève (and always finishing at the tomb, 'antique and simple' in form, of Jean-Jacques, on the Isle of Poplars). Nerval's is a landscape of castles and battlemented towers, red swaying masses of thicket on the green of valleys, orange gilding of sunsets. Trees, and more trees. Landscapes flat as slumber. Bluish morning mists making ghosts rise everywhere. October evenings made of old gold. You walk there as if in a dream, slowly, without effort (little steep or broken terrain). The rustle of dead leaves.

There's a feeling of melancholy in Nerval's attitude to walking. The melancholy of names and memories (present in Les Filles du Feu and in the Promenades). When walking, you end by reaching a hamlet. Crossing woodlands enveloped in fog, you come to the village bathed in autumn light. You'd been dreaming its name for ages: Cuffy, Châalis, Loisy, Othis ... The gentleness of melancholy: in a light that is always vague and unsteady, walking with Nerval cradles the mind, all tossed about by renascent memories. And through that, through those gentle, easy walks, the long sorrows of childhood are recalled. You only remember your dreams when walking.

That sort of walking, in those shivering forests, in a light changing from blue in the morning to orange in the evening, with nothing lively or trenchant to be seen, doesn't soothe sadness. It doesn't constitute its bracing remedy, its energy resource. It doesn't erase sadness, it transforms it. This is an alchemy that children know and practise: you walk as if you were letting yourself float in water, to dilute the sorrow and drown yourself in it. Let your sadness sail away in the free air; let yourself go. A dreamy walking, in which Nerval rediscovered the solitary stroller. Like Nietzsche (who always made you climb), at the pinnacle not of his destiny, but of his childish dreams.

'Hi-ho, a horseman, ho / Riding home from Flanders, oh ...' Old songs murmuring on the lips. Walking all day long in autumn, under a timid sun, leads to a blurring of times. Among these low hillocks the years are scattered, piled up, confused with each other. And always the same rustling, the same soughing wind, the same weak daylight. Childhood was the day before yesterday; yesterday, just now, this minute, maintaining that infinitely diluted sorrow along the dark, cool forest paths. Nerval has this quality of dreamy melancholy: slow rambles awakening ghosts from earlier times, kindly women's faces. And the certainty, when walking, of a childhood spent only and always in this light. Not nostalgia for lost years, nor nostalgia for child-hood, but childhood itself as nostalgia (only children know the miracle of *nostalgia without a past*). While walking there, slowly, in those Valois landscapes.

Otherwise there was the melancholia of *Aurélia*: active, sombre, given to *idées fixes*, to the completion of time. No longer the sympathetic, grave, languorous, autumnal strolling, but the fevered march of a quest, of destiny, the imminence of the end of time. From the summer of 1854, after leaving Dr Blanche's clinic (the doctor did not consider him cured), Nerval never stopped walking. He had a room in a wayside hotel, but only to sleep, not for long, when his exhausted body demanded rest. He walked and walked, would stop at a café, drink, and move on. He would stop at a reading-room or library, then visit a friend, then continue walking. Not flight, but a fixed insistence on confirming what is foreseen.

Walking had become part of an active melancholia. In *Aurélia* there is an image of walking that shows the signs everywhere. The anxious exaltation of the mad walker in towns. The streets are an excellent environment for maintaining, nourishing and deepening the illness. Everywhere sly glances, strange jerky movements, contradictory noises: engine sounds, bells, snatches of speech, the drumming of thousands of feet on the pavements. And as a route has to be found somehow, everything becomes a struggle and delirium is completed.

I am thinking of the last day, 25 January 1855: the final wander, which ended for Nerval in the rue de la Vieille-Lanterne where he found a window grille from which to hang himself. Not really a 'wander', on second thoughts, for he was pursuing a fixed, urgent idea. He had *Aurélia* in his legs. And whatever it is that makes a man follow a beckoning star.

When we examine his moments of intensity – deep despair or sudden euphoria, little to choose between them – we find a constant temptation to walk: must go out, must leave, must go and follow. You walk hurriedly, with the impression that people are everywhere staring at you, surrounding you, denouncing you, but you have to keep moving despite, against, the crowds with you and against you. Walking, as a continued decision of the illness, a lofty conquest of solitude. And you see that here everything scintillates, signals, calls out. Nerval saw a star growing bigger, the moon multiplying. Walking made his illness flower. It completed the madness, because while walking everything becomes *logical*: your legs bear the weight, and you think, that's it, must go there, it's good down there. Others think we are wandering aimlessly, when really it's a matter of following the idea, the idea that pulls, that carries us forward. Words come to the lips; we talk as we walk. Everything is true. Walking is a part of active melancholia.

'I was singing as I walked a mysterious anthem.' Melodies come back, confirming yet again. This walk no longer brings back gentle memories, rather it multiplies coincidences. A proliferation of signs: that's really it.

He found his way to that rue de la Vieille-Lanterne, very dark, unlighted, tiny, buried in back streets, hard to find. People 'fell on' it by taking the rue de la Tuerie, which started from the place du Châtelet. They had to follow that first alley until it narrowed. There it became a 'narrow, slimy, sinister' staircase, leading downward to the rue de la Vieille-Lanterne – a minuscule corner of dark pavement. To go there at night was the very 'idea of a descent into hell' (Dumas).

Did he die of the unbearable bitterness of restored lucidity, or of an extreme eruption of the illness, its consummation? Nerval was found hanged in the pale dawn ('his hat still on his head', according to Dumas, inspired as always by others' misfortunes).

But do we know why we walk?

18

A Daily Outing – Kant

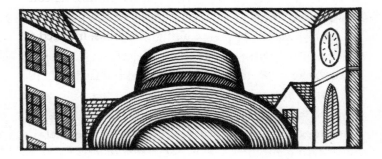

We know that Immanuel Kant's life was far from adventurous. It is hard to imagine a drearier existence. He was born in Königsberg and died there. He never travelled, never left his native town. His father made saddles and harnesses. His mother was very pious and loving. He never heard an insult uttered at home, but lost both parents at an early age. He studied, worked hard, became a tutor, then a lecturer, then a university professor. At the beginning of his first book is the statement: 'I have traced a path which I will follow. When my advance begins, nothing will be able to stop it.'

Of medium height, with a large head and bright blue eyes, the right shoulder higher than the left, he had a delicate constitution. He had gone blind in one eye. His behaviour was such a model of regularity that some called him 'the Königsberg clock'. On teaching days, when he emerged from his house, people knew it was exactly eight o'clock. At ten to, he had put on his hat; at five to, he had picked up his stick; and at dead on eight he stepped out of his door. He said of his watch that it was the last possession he would part with.

Like Nietzsche – although with different emphases – he was concerned with only two things apart from reading and writing: the importance of his walk, and what he should eat. But their styles differed absolutely. Nietzsche was a great, indefatigable walker, whose hikes were long and sometimes steep; and he usually ate sparingly, like a hermit, always trying out diets, seeking what would least upset his delicate stomach.

Kant by contrast had a good appetite, drank heartily, although not to excess, and spent long hours at the table. But he looked after himself during his daily walk which was always very brief, a bit perfunctory. He couldn't bear to perspire. So in summer he would walk very slowly, and stop in the shade when he began to overheat.

Of neither can it be said that his health was perfect. We should note – without seeing it as physiologically symbolic of their respective philosophies – that Kant was constipated, while Nietzsche suffered from compulsive vomiting. Of fragile temperament, Kant liked to think that he owed his longevity (he lived to be eighty) to his inflexible lifestyle. He held his good health to be a personal achievement, the product of his iron self-discipline. He was passionately interested in dietetic medicine, which (he said) was an art not for enjoying life but prolonging it.

In his final years, however, he claimed that an airborne electrical fluid had ruined his health, a current he also claimed had caused the death of an improbable number of cats in Basle at about the same time. He never had any debts, and said so very loudly to anyone who would listen. He couldn't bear untidiness. Things always had to be in their place. All change was unbearable to him.

A student who regularly attended his lectures had always had a button missing from his jacket. One day he turned up with a new button, which bothered the professor terribly: he could not prevent his gaze from straying back to the new button on the youngster's coat. Legend has it that Kant asked the student to remove the new button, adding that it is more important to learn a thing than it is to know, after learning it, where to classify it. He always dressed in the same way. He displayed no caprice or oddity.

His life was as exactly ruled as music manuscript paper. He was awoken each morning at five o'clock, never later. He breakfasted on a couple of bowls of tea, then smoked a pipe, the only one of the day. On teaching days, he would go out in the morning to give his lecture, then resume his dressing-gown and slippers to work and write until precisely a quarter to one. At that point he would dress again to receive, with enjoyment, a small group of friends to discuss science, philosophy and the weather.

There were invariably three dishes and some cheese,

placed on the table – sometimes with a few desserts – along with a small carafe of wine for each guest. Conversation lasted until five o'clock.

Then it was time for his walk. Rain or shine, it had to be taken. He went alone, for he wanted to breathe through his nose all the way, with his mouth closed, which he believed to be excellent for the body. The company of friends would have obliged him to open his mouth to speak.

He always took the same route, so consistently that his itinerary through the park later came to be called 'The Philosopher's Walk'. According to rumour he only ever altered the route of this daily constitutional twice in his life: to obtain an early copy of Rousseau's *Émile*, and to join the scramble for hot news after the announcement of the French Revolution. On returning from his walk, he read until ten o'clock, then went to bed (he only ate one meal a day), falling asleep immediately.

That low-key walk, without any big mystical union with Nature, that walk without pleasure, but taken as a hygienic necessity, that one-hour walk, but taken every day, every single day without exception, brings to light three important aspects of walking.

The first is monotony. Walking is monotonous, severely monotonous. The great walking narratives (from Rodolphe Töpffer's 'zigzag journeys' to Michel Vieuchange's 'travel logs') can only maintain our interest through their account of misadventures, sudden encounters, painful hardships. In these epics of pilgrimage or exploration, there are always many more pages devoted to halts than to the travelling itself. Events are never part of the walking, they are interruptions. For walking is monotonous by itself. It isn't 'interesting', and children know it. Basically, walking is always the same, putting one foot in front of the other. But the secret of that monotony is that it constitutes a remedy for boredom. Boredom is immobility of the body confronted with emptiness of mind. The repetitiveness of walking eliminates boredom, for, with the body active, the mind is no longer affected by its lassitude, no longer draws from its inertia the vague vertigo of an endless spiral. In a state of boredom one is always seeking *something to do*, despite the obvious futility of any activity. When walking, there is always something to do: walk. Or rather, no, there's nothing more to do because one is just walking, and when one is going to a place or covering a route, one has only to keep moving. That is boringly obvious. The body's monotonous duty liberates thought. While walking, one is not obliged to think, to think this or that or like this or like that. During that continuous but automatic effort of the body, the mind is placed at one's disposal. It is then that thoughts can *arise*, surface or take shape.

The second aspect pivots around regularity. What impresses in Kant is his iron discipline. Every day that same walk, the accompaniment and symbol of the hours spent working each day. Every day a page to write, a thought to develop, a proof to add, a demonstration to perfect. And at the end of it all, a gigantic oeuvre. Of course, he also had to have something to think and say in the first place. But what impresses here is the output, the idea of a gigantism produced through repeated effort, a small repeated action: a discipline. The work was not produced in a flash of inspiration suspending time, but built up stone by stone. As when, after three or four days' walk, you look back from the top of a pass and make out in the far distance your point of departure. That distance, that remoteness stolen by the tiny distance of a stride, one stride after another, with unending perseverance. Discipline is the impossible conquered by the obstinate repetition of the possible.

The third and last aspect has to do with the inescapable. It was known that at five in the afternoon he was going to come out and take his walk. It was like an immutable ritual, as regular and fundamental as the sunrise. What the idea of the inescapable adds to that of regularity is inevitability, but a mastered inevitability that one imposes *by means of*. Through discipline it can happen that one becomes one's own destiny. There is a sort of threshold of the will, which, at the end of twenty, thirty or forty years, bends our efforts towards a necessity that would hang over us, almost, if we were not preoccupied with its construction.

The inescapable is there to show that discipline is not only a passive habit. It makes us feel a destiny of will, through which Nietzsche defined freedom. The inescapable thing about walking is that once started, one is forced to arrive. There is no other way, one has to progress. And at the end of the fatigue and the road, one *always* arrives, it's enough to add up the hours and think: *Let's go!* It was written, unchangeable. When you are on foot, to arrive you must walk. Will as destiny.

19

Strolls

Of course you walk during leisurely strolls. During a promenade or stroll, the act of walking lacks the density of long excursions, but other dimensions can be felt, more humble, less suited to grand mystical poses, metaphysical frauds and pretentious declarations. They are: the promenade as an absolute ritual, the creation of a childish soul; the promenade as free relaxation, mental recreation; the promenade as rediscovery.

The outings of our childhood were a ritual. They required well-trodden routes, strictly bounded time-tables. Not just going out for a random stroll, not just *an* outing, but *this* or *that* outing. To children, they don't seem similar in the least. They take different paths, the hedges that line them are unique, as are the views. They don't intersect.

Growing up means becoming sensitive only to generalities, to similarities, to genres of being. Forests, mountains, plains. In your own neighbourhood, too, everything becomes alike: to us adults, each path is bound up, contained, in the same broad landscape. The adult sees everything from the height of his years. The outlook born of experience flattens everything, piles it together, renders it dull. It all comes down to the same. He knows his house is situated in a country, and that several roads lead to it.

To a child, roads have an intimidating, unnerving side, they are potential different worlds. They do not resemble one another: they open onto distinct universes. The child has already noticed that no two trees are the same: their knotty branches, their twisted trunks, their outlines all differentiate them. Not two mulberries or two oaks, but the knight and the wizard, the monster and the child. So what can be said about two outings, each with its unique succession of trees, of characters, the colours of its paths, the people one might meet there? Each outing has a separate story, each opens into a different kingdom, differently inhabited, differently haunted.

Proust as a child had two outings that made two worlds: by Swann's house (or by Méséglise), and to Guermantes: maps of two complete worlds, with their seasons, their sounds, their duration, their colours. Thus, by Swann's house was the outing risked even in threatening weather since it was

short, the festoons of lilacs to be gently embraced, the haw-
thorns with their intoxicating scent, Swann's park where
sometimes there might appear from between hedges of
jasmine, the scoffing young girl Gilberte, impenetrable
and wily.

The Guermantes outing involved leaving by the back
door at the end of the garden, and needed reliable weather
because it led far off. Guermantes was essentially a fabulous
destination, never reached, but the walk passed the banks
of the Vivonne (where one could sometimes sit down beside
the water, among irises), and that house buried in the woods
on whose windowsill an elegant woman, sad and pensive,
sometimes leaned her elbow. And there were small damp
clearings where 'clusters of dark flowers' climbed.

Two separate worlds. Albertine, much later, was to shock
the Narrator by suggesting that they go to Guermantes by
way of Méséglise ... Scandal, aberration, horrors! The objective realities of geography smash head-on into the clean,
crystalline perceptions of childhood. To a child, an outing is
a complete identity, a face, an individual. It isn't routes that
intersect at a junction, or paths under an unchanging sky.
Doubtless it was possible, from the belfry of Saint-Hilaire,
to make out the routes of both outings at once, from a
single viewpoint, bathed in the colour of a single landscape,
a single light. But that overview is falsely superior, of interest only to an abstract gaze seeing roads as lines on a map.
A child, who lives at ground level, knows that the shapes of
the stones, the outlines of the trees, the scents of the flowers,
are all different.

And we oughtn't to be contrasting the imaginative, dreamy outlook of children with the realism and objectivity of adults. It is children who are the true realists: they never proceed from generalities. The adult recognizes the general form in a particular example, a representative of the species, dismisses everything else and states: that's lilac, there's an ash tree, an apple tree. The child perceives individuals, personalities. He sees the unique form, and doesn't mask it with a common name or function. When you walk with children, they enable you to see the fabulous beasts in tree foliage, to smell the sweetness of blossoms. It isn't a triumph of the imagination, but an unprejudiced, total realism. And Nature becomes instantly poetic. These outings are the absolute reign of childhood. You lose its charm in growing up, because you end by acquiring ideas and certainties about everything, and no longer want to know more of things than their objective representation (sadly called their 'truth').

Well beyond childhood, there exists a style of outing that is just as dreamy, although less poetic. I refer to the stroll as light relief, relaxation: walking to 'get some fresh air'. After a gruelling work session, or when the boredom becomes too much, people go off for a walk to 'have a think'. Especially when the contrast becomes too strong between a spring sun, brisk air outside and the stuffy, gloomy atmosphere of an office. A German philosopher described this art tactfully and with great precision.

In *Die Promenade als Kunstwerk* ('The Art of Walking', 1802), Karl Gottlob Schelle effectively established that walking undoubtedly produced a relaxing effect on the body – literally so, since, free of the crouching posture imposed by work, it could stand up straight; but it was really the mind that rejoiced most. For walking does bring a sort of relaxation to the soul. While working, you have to remain the captive of your subject, stay shackled to your task, think of only one thing at a time. The seated body can't move about much, and when engaged in effort must keep its movements exact, the working of its muscles coordinated. In this way work always results in a state of nervous irritation, due to forced and prolonged concentration.

Nevertheless, a walk doesn't signify a quick rest, a simple pause, as if it were simply a matter of *stopping*. It is rather a matter of a change in rhythm: it unshackles the body's limbs along with the mind's faculties. Walking in the first place means defying the constraints: choosing your route, your pace and your representations. Schelle was said to be a friend of Kant. One can also tell that he read his work: he comes up with a complete Kantian aesthetic, applied to walking.

An outing is not the same thing as a brisk trot around the block, which is really just another way of developing the obsession with some idea or the thread of a meditation. After all, I can easily get up and walk about when I am held up by a problem. But then I don't necessarily go far, I take a few paces, hands behind back and shaking my head, and as soon as the motion of the body has given a little more spring to the mind – solving the problem, finding the ideal arrangement, building the correct demonstration, seizing the good idea – then I rush back to my desk, until the next blockage.

Going out for a walk is another matter: you say goodbye to your work. You close the books and files, and you go out. Once outside, the body moves at its own rhythm and the mind feels free, in other words, available. I turn my head towards the impressions that attract me to the right side of the landscape, I harmonize them with the ones I receive from the left, I play with colour contrasts, I pass from detail to overall view in a continuous back-and-forth scanning process. And if I am on an ample walk in a public park already filled with a motley crowd, I observe, but without the mind being applied: I let my gaze slide from one face to another, from a dress to a hat, without allowing myself to be caught anywhere, never retaining more than a shape, a line, an expression. It is that free composition of the theatre of appearances that Kant calls aesthetic pleasure: the imagination playing with impressions, combining and recomposing them at the whim of one's unfettered fantasy. It's totally gratuitous, and by that means the mind displays its deep internal harmony: all the faculties in spontaneous agreement to play freely together at putting the spectacle of the world into proper form.

For the art of walking to be practised to the full, Schelle specifies, a number of external conditions have to be present. If you promenade in public places, wide paths or walks are needed, so that passers-by are not perpetually obstructed by others, and the crowd should be neither too dense nor too thin: if there are only a few other strollers you will be tempted to seek recognizable faces and peer at them (is that him?), which will bring you back to your social roles. If there are too many, you will be discouraged by the torrent of multiple images which will overburden your capacity for synthesis. If you choose the countryside, you need a landscape containing mountains, valleys, streams, plains and woods, to entertain the imagination with a diversity of colours and shapes, and preferably a radiant sun, for without it the play of the imagination may be weighed down with gloomy representations.

Apart from all that, it's absolutely essential to alternate urban and country walks, without favouring one over the other. For while they share a common basis (free play of the imagination in recomposing impressions), their qualities are different: walking on pavements and park alleys involves a casual approach, giving access, via the diversity of humanity and of the behaviour of our fellows, to detailed small discoveries, enchanting to the mind; walking alone in the company of streams and trees is more likely to produce a dreamy state, very far removed from the stresses of systematic introspection, but by the same token, fertile: as if, gently distracted by the sight of flowers and skylines, the soul could forget itself for a while, and thus become aware of some facets of its own that ordinarily stay hidden.

The secret of the promenade is that availability of the mind, so rare in our busy, polarized lives, imprisoned in our own stubbornness. 'Availability' is a rare synthesis of abandon and activity, deploying all the charm of the mind during a walk. The soul becomes as it were available to the world of appearances. It has nothing to explain to anyone, and no obligation to be coherent. And in that game without consequences, it may be that the world yields more of itself to the whimsical saunterer than to the serious and systematic observer.

These discoveries and joys can only be given to those who stroll with an open mind. They should never be sought deliberately for themselves, as if sauntering were a method. They will come spontaneously to one who, summoned by spring sunshine, joyously abandons his work just to get a little time to himself. One who goes out with a light heart, and a wish to put aside for a moment his labours and his fate. Only thus – with no expectation of a specific profit from the outing, and with all cares and worries firmly left behind in desk drawers – will a stroll become that gratuitous aesthetic moment, that rediscovery of the lightness of being, the sweetness of a soul freely reconciled to itself and to the world.

Of course the art of strolling is a recreational technique. But that sort of recreation can also be a literal *re-creation*, particularly in town. Usually people walk the streets in a thoroughly practical manner, to go for bread, to the shops, to the bus or subway, to drop in on a friend. Then, streets are just corridors. People walk with their heads down, recognizing only what they need to. They look at nothing, they navigate, perceiving only the functional minimum: turn right at the green pharmacy sign, that big brown gateway means the bakery is on the next corner. Thus the street becomes a mere tissue of feeble, twinkling signs, with its spectacle largely extinguished.

One needs to give oneself the treat – unusual but easy – of walking in one's own neighbourhood, walking there with a hesitant, irregular pace, deciding to take a stroll there for no reason, slowly, with eyes raised for once. That is when the prodigy happens. Just walking, without rush, without any set purpose, makes the town look a little as it might have looked to one seeing it for the first time. With no focus on anything in particular, everything is offered in abundance: colours, details, shapes, aspects. Strolling, walking alone and without purpose, restores that vision: the colour of those shutters, the slash of colour they make on the walls; the delicate black arabesques of window grilles; the comically differing houses, tall and narrow like stone giraffes or low and broad like stout turtles; the construction of windows, bright orange reflecting the sunset against mottled grey façades. One can plunder the streets delicately like that for ages.

20

Public Gardens

There is one circumstance, however, that makes a stroll collapse back into worldly artifice, instead of unveiling the aesthetic essence of streets or countryside. I refer here to the sort of gallant, stylish saunter taken mainly to be seen. Its Parisian symbol is unarguably the Tuileries Gardens, which Corneille referred to as 'the land of fine folk and gallantry' (*The Liar*). Nature is absolutely dominated there: dead-straight, clipped box hedges, rectilinear walks, strictly pruned trees, artificial fountains, lascivious statues.

Originally only high society was allowed in, entry being denied to the rabble and the crowd of cursing lackeys waiting at the entrance for their mistresses to finish playing the sweetie-pie among swooning suitors. Still, 'milliners' – working-class good-time girls – were admitted so long as they were well-dressed, pretty or in respectable company. In summer, people stayed there until late, in the orange light and violet reflections, the sweetness of the evening advancing on tiptoe, and the dust thrown up by thousands of footsteps. The trees are still scarred with women's names, carved by sad lovers.

> Allons aux Tuilleries,
> Entretenir tantost nos tristes resveries.
> (*Let's go to the Tuileries*
> *Soon to pursue our sad fantasies.*)

It was a place much favoured by young girls in the flower of beauty, married women on the lookout for adventure, and widows seeking consolation. For it is an unspeakable bore to a woman to have but a single man – her husband – before her eyes. The gardens answered that need as noted by Charles Sorel in his 1648 tale, *Polyandre*: 'Most women of spirit greatly loved the Cours and walking in the Luxembourg or the Tuileries, being well content to see new men there every day.' It was the height of bad taste to go there as a couple, husband and wife.

People dawdled in the wide main walks of the gardens, stopping (or rather striking a pose) from time to time, but not through any political resistance to speed. It was more that only slowness enabled people to ogle at their leisure, display their finery and charms, and show how much wit they had. Of course, meticulous care was lavished on appearance (for nothing could be forgiven, nothing could be got away with: 'The faces there are masterpieces of art / in which nature has often had not the least part', according to the Harlequin Evaristo Gherardi), and companions carefully chosen (to avoid tiresome individuals who might spoil gallant encounters), and off they went: Parisiennes in all their glory.

Why did they walk? La Bruyère thought he knew: 'to show off a beautiful fabric and reap the fruits of their toilette'. The real beauties trailed murmurs of rapture in their wake. But what they did couldn't really be called walking; it was more a sophisticated gait, a studied swaying. As recommended by a servant addressing her mistress in Gherardi's 1695 *Promenades de Paris*:

> Like all the beauties, don't risk a natural approach here. Be you with me in the Broad Walk, for example: you must speak to me while saying nothing, the better to seem witty, laugh for no reason the better to appear playful, draw yourself up at every moment to show your bosom, open your eyes wide to make them bigger, bite your lips to redden them.

So we could start with the Grande Allée, the Great Walk, which is like the main stage on which people fight to see and be seen, judge and be judged:

> It's the quarry of fine society.
> It's there, with great array,
> As the sun begins to set,
> That both brunette and blonde themselves display,
> It's there they make a show
> Of fabrics and ribbons and lace.

171

It's there that all the amblers
Come to auction their figure and their face.
It's there they treat themselves to a public tryst,
That all objects are found
And that all disdain the rest
Because they are all alike.

But there were other small stages, transverse walks each
with its own speciality: on the east side was a row of benches
where people could 'slander at their ease' (the critics' and
curmudgeons' walk), while other more shadowy walks were
known for secret rendezvous, and yet others seemed gentle
and sad, welcoming to melancholics.

The variety of showcases made the Tuileries into a play in
which all were actors and spectators. As in a theatre, all types
could be seen there: the beauty obsessed with her outfit,
the ridiculous ladies' man, the pompous and arrogant
magistrate, the strutting officer, the pseudo-intellectual,
the bourgeois, the young fop, the former seminarian, the
rumour-spreading 'gossipmonger' from whom the latest
lie could be heard, and then of course a few drunkards. But
everyone stood as tall as possible, displayed their wares,
meagre or sumptuous, and glanced discreetly about to see
what effect they were producing on others. People wore
false calves to disguise skinny shanks, put on false faces,
flashed their diamonds, raised their voices.

In that permanent merry-go-round people sought,
ignored and assessed one another, and strove to have an air
(happy or sad: but you had to have one). Behind the differences, as the poem says, they were 'all alike'. Meaning, once

again, that they were all exchanging extravagant compliments while secretly despising one another, mocking one another reciprocally:

> A grotesque who sees sideways
> Will ridicule a one-eyed man.
> An ass laughs at a drunkard, a cuckold at a bastard,
> Each woman at her partner.

And in that concert of murmured banter, intrigues were set up: people made appointments, pretended to have met by chance, followed girls they didn't know, got into conversation; women dropped their gloves, young fellows ran to kneel at their feet ... It was the great 'time of the Tuileries'.

21

The Urban Flâneur

In his reflections on Paris, Walter Benjamin spotlighted the character of the flâneur, far removed from the ogling Tuileries gallant. He analysed, described and captured him from a rereading of Baudelaire – Le Spleen de Paris, the 'Tableaux parisiens' in Les Fleurs du mal, the sketches in Vie moderne. This form of strolling presupposes three elements, or the presence of three conditions: city, crowd, and capitalism.

The urban flâneur does experience walking, but in a way far removed from Nietzsche or Thoreau. Walking in town is torture to the lover of long rambles in nature, because it imposes, as we shall see, an interrupted, uneven rhythm. But the fact remains that the flâneur *walks*, unlike the mere loafer, always stopping to see the attraction or stare entranced into shop windows. The flâneur walks, he makes his way even through the crowd.

Strolling requires those urban concentrations that developed in the nineteenth century, so dense and unbroken that you can walk for hours without seeing a piece of country. Walking through these new megalopolises (Berlin, London, Paris), you passed through districts that were like different worlds, separate, apart. Everything could vary: the size and architectural style of the buildings, the quality and scent of the air, the way of living, the ambiance, the light, the social topography. The flâneur appeared at a time when the city had acquired enough scale to become a landscape. It could be crossed as if it were a mountain, with its passes, its reversals of viewpoint, its dangers and surprises too. It had become a forest, a jungle.

The second element behind the appearance of the flâneur was the crowd. He strolled among the crowd and through it. That crowd in which he developed had already become *the masses*: labouring, nameless, bustling. In the great industrial cities, those people on the way to or from work, going to business meetings, rushing to deliver a package or get to a rendezvous, were representatives of the new civilization. This crowd was *hostile*, hostile to all its members. Everyone was in a hurry and everyone else was in their way. The crowd transformed the other instantly into a competitor.

This crowd wasn't that of the people on the march, the crowd of big demonstrations, of united demands; the epic mob, that formidable mass of collective energy. On the contrary, everyone in it showed contradictory interests, on the concrete level of their movement from place to place. No one met anyone. Unknown faces, generally forbidding, statistically unlikely to be known. The common experience of preceding centuries had been surprise at the sight of a *stranger* in town, an unknown face. Where's he from, what's he up to? Now, anonymity was the norm. The shock would be to recognize someone. In the crowd, the basic codes of the encounter vanish completely. Out of the question to say 'Good day', or stop and exchange a word or two on the weather.

Thirdly, capitalism; or more exactly, what Benjamin saw as the reign of merchandise. For him, capitalism designated the moment when the concept of merchandise extended beyond industrial products, to include art works and people. The mercantilization of the world: everything becomes a consumer product, everything is bought and sold, available on the great market of endless demand. The reign of generalized prostitution, of selling, and selling yourself.

~

The urban stroller is *subversive*. He subverts the crowd, the merchandise and the town, along with their values. The walker of wide-open spaces, the trekker with his rucksack opposes civilization with the burst of a clean break, the cutting edge of a rejection (Jack Kerouac, Gary Snyder, etc.). The stroller's walking activity is more ambiguous, his resistance to modernity ambivalent. Subversion is not a matter of opposing but of evading, deflecting, altering with exaggeration, accepting blandly and moving rapidly on. The flâneur subverts solitude, speed, dubious business politics and consumerism.

Solitude first: the isolating effect of crowds has often been described. An unending succession of strangers' faces, a thick blanket of indifference which deepens moral solitude. No one feels he knows anyone else, and the mass presence of this feeling produces a dense hostility, making the individual prey to everyone. The stroller seeks this anonymity because he *hides* in it. He melts into the mechanical mass, but voluntarily, to conceal himself there. After that, anonymity is not a constraint that crushes him, but an opportunity for enjoyment, enabling him to feel more vividly himself from his private internal vantage point. Since he is hiding, he won't experience anonymity as oppression, but as opportunity. Amid the dense, gloomy solitude of the crowd, he carves out that of an observer and poet: *no one can see what he is looking at!* He is like a wrinkle in the crowd. The stroller is *out of synch*, a decisive maladjustment that without excluding or distancing him, abstracts him from the anonymous mass and makes him singular *in himself*.

Next, speed. In the crowd everyone is pressed, in two ways: in a hurry, and constantly obstructed. But the stroller doesn't have to go anywhere in particular. So he can stop for any incident or display, scrutinize interesting faces, slow down for intersections. But resisting the speed of business politics, his slowness becomes the condition for a higher agility: that of the mind. For he grasps images on the wing. The hastening passer-by combines velocity of the body with degradation of the intellect. He wants only to go fast and his mind is empty, preoccupied with slipping through the interstices. The flâneur's body moves slowly, but his eyes dart about and his mind is gripped by a thousand things at once.

With regard to the convoluted relations between business and politics, government increasingly by and for big capital, Benjamin's stroller was absolutely impervious to the ambient productivism and the utilitarianism behind it. He was himself useless, and his idleness condemned him to marginal status. Nevertheless he never remained wholly passive. He might do nothing, but he followed everything, observing, his mind always alert. And by catching collisions and encounters in flight, he created a flow of poetic images. If the stroller didn't exist, everyone would follow their own course, produce their own series of phenomena, and there would be no one to report what was going on at street corners. The stroller noted sparks, frictions, encounters.

Lastly, consumption, consumerism. The crowd is the experience of a commoditized future in formation. Tossed about and dragged along by it, the individual is reduced to being a mere product offered up to anonymous tides. Offered up, going with the flow. In a crowd, there's always this impression of being effectively consumed: by the movements that constrain the body, the paroxysms that shake it. One is consumed by the streets, the boulevards. The signs and shop windows are only there to boost the circulation and exchange of goods. The stroller does not consume and is not consumed. He practises urban foraging, or even theft. He does not, in the manner of the walker of the plains or mountains, receive the landscape as a gift for his effort. But he captures, snatches in flight implausible encounters, furtive moments, fleeting coincidences. He doesn't consume, but nevertheless continues to capture vignettes, to bring down on himself a drizzle of images stolen in the improbable instant of the encounter.

Yet this poetic creativity retains an ambiguous quality: it is, Benjamin said, a 'fantasmagoria'. It bypasses the awfulness of the city to recapture its passing marvels, it explores the poetry of collisions, but without stopping to denounce the alienation of labour and the masses. The flâneur has better things to do: remythologize the city, invent new divinities, explore the poetic surface of the urban spectacle.

Baudelairean sauntering spawned a number of descendants. There was the surrealist meandering that gave the stroller's art two new dimensions: chance and night (Louis Aragon at the Buttes-Chaumont in Paris Peasant, André Breton crazily seeking love in Nadja). Then there was the Situationist 'drift' theorized by Guy Debord: sensitive exploration of differences (being transformed by ambiances). The question that now arises is whether the spread of uniform brands ('chains' as we call them without irony, identical links, tightening around us) and the aggressive expansion of traffic haven't made urban strolling more difficult, less delightful and surprising. Spaces where strolling is compulsory are being made, but no one has to go there.

The great romantic walker, the eternal wanderer, communed with the Essence. Walking was a ceremony of mystic union, the walker being co-present with the Presence, curled up in the pure bosom of a maternal Nature. In both Rousseau and Wordsworth we find walking celebrated as testimony to presence and mystical fusion. What is retained in Wordsworth's well-turned verse and Rousseau's musical prose is precisely that deep unhurried breathing, that gentleness of rhythm.

The urban stroller doesn't put in an appearance at the fullness of Essence, he just lays himself open to scattered visual impacts. The walker is fulfilled in an abyss of fusion, the stroller in a firework-like explosion of successive flashes.

22

Gravity

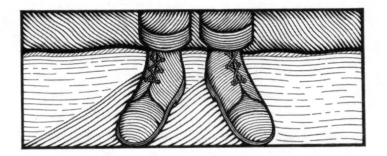

I keep forgetting those short blessed moments, sometimes due to great tiredness, those brief ecstatic
instants when the body, while walking, advances
without being aware of itself, almost like a tumbling
dead leaf. Especially after a long walk when the fatigue is
immense, and you suddenly lose all sensation. Then, as long
as the path is well enough laid out and not too steep, you
stop looking down, stop thinking altogether, and let your
feet find the right places and avoid the pitfalls.

On the walker's side, there's nothing left but an immense
renunciation. The walk ends in a sort of dream, and the tread
then gains in firmness and speed. As soon as you consent to
stop thinking. After that, you can't call it lightness because

you no longer feel a thing: your legs are absorbed by the road and your mind *floats overhead*. Now, when you run for long enough, the time comes when you feel a huge impression of lightness, as if carried off in a race of your own. After a period, sometimes a long one, of 'finding your pace', at last the body finds its breathing rhythm and your feet answer the rhythmic *call* to rebound from the road, like a regular, repeated take-off. The experience of lightness when running is still wholly distinct from the feeling of induced lightness that walking can, on rare occasions, produce. It isn't the intoxication you feel on a run, from the perfect tension of the muscles, but more a mental detachment produced by tiredness, a creeping anaesthesia. The lightness felt in running is really an unfatiguing victory over gravity, an easy and sovereign assertion of the body. The floating feeling derived from walking comes when the feet have ultimately become one with the road, and the mind through lassitude *forgets* to echo their fatigue.

The fact remains that, very broadly speaking, the experience of walking is always a perception of gravity. I don't exactly mean that of a heavy, weighty body. Even if sometimes, truth to tell, when there are still several hours to go before the end of the stage, and the path steepens, your knees might just as well be carrying an anvil. What I am trying to get at is what runs all through those immense days in the open: at every step, contact, the foot endlessly falling back down; that support every time, the perpetual sinking down to lift up again. You have to take root each time so that you can depart anew. That is how the foot takes root, through that repeated enlacement with the earth. Each step forming another knot. There is no way of being more earthbound than by walking: the immeasurable monotony of the soil.

I think of those abstracted sedentary individuals who spend their lives in an office rattling their fingers on a keyboard: 'connected', as they say, but to what? To information mutating between one second and the next, floods of images and numbers, pictures and graphs. And after work it's the subway, the train, always speed, the gaze now glued to the telephone screen, more touches and strokes and messages scrolling past, images ... and night falls, when they still haven't seen anything of the day. Television, another screen. What dimension do they live in, without dust raised by movement, without contact, in what featureless space, in what time, where neither rain nor shine count? Those lives, disconnected from roads and routes, make them forget our condition, as if erosion by changing weather over time didn't exist.

A Taoist sage said: 'Feet on the ground occupy very little space; it's through all the space they don't occupy that we can walk.' Which means in the first place that people don't keep still. Watch a man waiting on his feet, poorly set: he prances, tramples, quickly feels chafed. He doesn't know what to do with his arms, swinging them weakly or clamping them against his body: he's in unstable equilibrium. When he starts to walk it all comes back immediately: nature unfolds, expresses itself, the wellspring of being relaxes, the rhythm resumes. The foot finds the right balance.

185

Zhuang Zhu also meant that the feet as such are small pieces of space, but their vocation ('walking') is to articulate the world's space. The size of the foot, the gap between the legs, have no role, are never lined up anywhere. But they measure all the rest. Our feet form a compass that has no useful function, apart from evaluating distance. The legs survey. Their stride constitutes a serviceable measurement.

In the end, to say that it's through what remains to me of the journey that I can walk makes obvious reference to the Taoist void: that void that isn't empty nothingness but pure virtuality, a void creating inspiration and *play*, like the play of letters and sounds that makes the life of words. Walking in that way *articulates* the depths of the space and brings the landscape to *life*.

To end, I would note that in many sporting activities, joy comes from the transgression of gravity, from victory over it through speed, height, vigour, the invitation to go ever higher. Walking on the other hand is to experience gravity at every step, the inexorable attraction of the earth's mass. The passage from running to rest is a violence. You hold your sides, you pour with sweat, your face is scarlet. You stop because the body's giving way, you're out of breath. When you walk, on the other hand, stopping is like a natural completion: you stop to welcome a new perspective, to breathe in the landscape. And then when you start off again, there isn't a break. It's more like a continuity between walking and rest, not a matter of transgressing gravity, but completing it.

Thus, walking reminds us constantly of our finiteness: bodies heavy with unmannerly needs, nailed to the definitive ground. Walking doesn't mean raising yourself, it doesn't mean getting the better of gravity, or letting speed and height delude you on your mortal condition; it means reconciling yourself to it through that exposure to the mass of the ground, the fragility of the body, the slow, remorseless sinking movement. Walking means precisely resigning yourself to being an ambulant, forward-leaning body. But the really astonishing thing is how that slow resignation, that immense lassitude give us the joy of being. Of being no more than that, of course, but in utter bliss. Our leaden bodies fall back to earth at every step, as if to take root there again. Walking is an invitation to die standing up.

23

Elemental

When setting out to walk for more than a few
days, say more than a week, one question
keeps arising as you pack your rucksack: is
this thing really necessary? A matter of weight, of course.
Because while we have been able to list the forms of well-
being it brings, walking can be a nightmare if you are
overloaded. So the same question, over and over: do I *really*
need this? Because you have to reduce as much as possible. Medicines and first aid, toiletries, clothing, food,
sleeping equipment, always the same obsession with elimi-
nating the superfluous, throwing out the useless. Just
take what you need to walk and stay alive. All you need
to walk is protection against cold and hunger. None of

the clobber normally taken to *kill time* while travelling is needed here.

'As if you could kill time without injuring eternity,' Thoreau wrote. You don't walk to kill time but to welcome it, to pick off its leaves and petals one by one, second by second. Anything that would help kill time, counteract boredom, divert the body and the mind, is much too heavy. In sorting out what to take and what to leave, no preoccupation with effect, no consideration of appearances, even of comfort or style, no social calculation should play any part. All that counts is a certain strict relation between weight and efficiency. All you need when walking is the necessary. Walking means living a life scoured bare (social varnish burned off), unburdened, divested of social skills, purged of futility and masks.

The necessary is on a level below the useful. The useful is something that intensifies a power to act, augments a production of effects or increases a competence. The useless or superfluous is whatever remains subject to the appreciation of others or to one's own vanity.

Just below the useful, there is the necessary.* Whatever is irreplaceable, indispensable, un-substitutable, anything whose absence will promptly be rewarded with some blockage, an involuntary halt, physical discomfort. Strong

---

* The distinction made here between the necessary and the elemental is not a rephrasing of the one made earlier in reference to the Cynics. The Cynics attempted to make the two notions work separately and show how each one demolished the classical dualities (appearance and essence, useful and futile). This time the elemental is considered as going beyond the necessary and the useful.

shoes, weatherproof or spare garments, provisions, first aid kit, maps ... For the merely useful there are nearly always natural equivalents: branches (for stakes, staffs, walking sticks), grasses (towels, bedding).

The bottom level is that of the elemental. It is almost a reversal. I recall one time in the Cévennes, at the foot of a mountain: still six or seven hours of walking to reach the summit. The weather was fine and settled, and the nights still warm. I made my decision there and then, and stuck my rucksack in the crotch of a tree. Nothing left on my shoulders or in my pockets. Two days like that followed, without anything. The sensation was one of immense lightness, relieved of even the necessary, without the very minimum: nothing. So there would be nothing between me and the sky, me and the ground (cool stream water from cupped hands; wild strawberries and bilberries; the soft ground for a couch).

The elemental is revealed as fullness of presence. And the necessary is distinct from the useful. The elemental no longer opposes: it is everything to the man who has nothing. The elemental is the primary, primitive layer, whose consistency can hardly be felt, for it yields itself in pure form only to one who has, at some time, got rid of the necessary. Walking, sometimes, for moments, lets you feel it. Otherwise, to reach it demands a brutal, dangerous, extreme conversion.

Here we should again draw the distinction between confidence as assurance and confidence as trust. Assurance comes from knowing you've got *the necessary*, the wherewithal to cope – with bad weather, paths in all directions, absence of water sources, cold nights. You feel you can count on your equipment, your experience, your capacity to anticipate. This the assurance of technologized man, who can master situations. Wily, responsible.

To walk without even the necessary is to *abandon yourself* to the elements. When you do that, nothing counts any more, plans, self-assurance, nothing. Nothing but a full and wholesale trust in the world's generosity. Stones, sky, earth, trees, all become subsidiary to us, a gift, inexhaustibly supportive. By abandoning ourselves to it we gain a previously unknown confidence which satisfies the heart, because it makes us totally dependent on an Other, relieving us even of the duty of self-preservation. The elemental is that to which we entrust ourselves, and which is given to us in its entirety. But to experience its texture we have to take a risk, the risk of going beyond the necessary.

24

Mystic and Politician – Gandhi

We are not going to turn back.

M. K. Gandhi, 10 March 1930

In December 1920, Gandhi predicted Indian independence for 'next year', if everyone followed the path he had mapped out for liberation from British rule: non-cooperation extending gradually into all sectors of activity, civil disobedience in progressive stages, pursuit of ever-increasing economic autarchy, and above all a refusal to respond violently to the repressive acts that would inevitably accompany that seditious campaign. After making this prediction, Gandhi travelled the length and breadth of India, preached traditional cotton-weaving methods, and organized bonfires to burn imported fabrics.

But the British stood firm, and the main effect of that incautious announcement from the Mahatma ('Great Soul') was to unleash a huge wave of arrests. Nevertheless civil disobedience had made a good start, and here and there the instructions were followed: strike pickets to be placed outside alcohol outlets, imported textiles to be boycotted, court summonses to be ignored. But eventually violence broke out and, after a confrontation with the forces of order causing deaths among the demonstrators, an angry mob set fire to a barracks, burning some twenty policemen alive. Gandhi reacted as he had to the Amritsar massacre in 1919: he called a halt to the civil disobedience movement and decided on a personal fast – a gesture he made a number of times in his life – assuming personal responsibility for the deaths, and exculpating the violent rioters.

A decade later (after a spell in jail, and a resumption of his long peregrinations in India campaigning against the exclusion of Untouchables, promoting women's rights and teaching basic hygiene), Gandhi in January 1930 again decided to defy the Empire, and launched a new non-cooperation campaign. But he was less confident in his approach this time, unsure of how to start, how to give the most publicity to a calm and massive refusal to obey. He confessed to the great poet Rabindranath Tagore, who visited him on 18 January: 'I see no light among the shadows that surround me.'

What he called his 'small voice' soon spoke up, though, telling him to march to the sea and gather salt. Gandhi had decided on a new *satyagraha:* the march for salt. The strategy was a double one: to denounce the salt tax, as the prelude to a more radical dissidence, and to stage the condemnation in the form of an immense mass march. The British held a monopoly on harvesting salt. No one was permitted to trade in it or even extract some for personal use. There was even recourse to destruction of deposits when natural salt was found close to populations who might take it for their own use. Salt: a free gift from the sea, a humble but indispensable foodstuff. The injustice of the tax was immediately obvious to all, and simply stating it was enough to underline its scandalous unfairness. The second stroke of genius was the organization of a slow mass march to the coast: a walk from the ashram[†] at Sabarmati to the Dandi salt marshes, on the seashore near Jalapur.

Gandhi had long valued the spiritual and political benefits of walking. In London, as a very young man, he had walked regularly, five to fifteen kilometres most days, attending his law lectures and finding vegetarian restaurants. Those walks helped him to live up to the three vows he had made to his mother when leaving India (no women, no alcohol, no meat), to test their solidity and measure his own constancy. Gandhi had always set great store by vows made to himself or others, those formal commitments to give up

---

[*] As we shall see later, this expression, meaning roughly 'truth-force', designates a collective action undertaken in determined fashion but rejecting in advance any recourse to violence.

[†] This term designates communal structures, organized around rules and principles based on his thought, that Gandhi had set up to further his work and train disciples.

this or that practice, this or that behaviour. He could only see them as final. And he had always cultivated personal discipline and self-control. Walking facilitates that decided relation with the self which is not of the order of undefined introspection (something better suited to a reclining posture on a sofa), but of meticulous self-examination.

While walking, you hold yourself to account: you correct yourself, challenge yourself, assess yourself. Later, working as a lawyer in South Africa, Gandhi continued to walk, regularly covering the thirty-four kilometres between the Tolstoy farm and Johannesburg. In the struggle he led in Natal, he again tried out a political dimension of walking. While defending the rights of South African Indians subjected to vexatious measures or unjust taxes, in 1913 he organized, instead of simple demonstrations to occupy public space, a number of marches several days long. The idea was to protest without violence, while trying to get arrested. Gandhi decided to organize marches leading from one province to another (Natal to the Transvaal) without obtaining the compulsory travel pass, thus mounting civil disobedience on a massive and visible scale, but collective and peaceful. On 13 October 1913, Gandhi accordingly took the lead of an immense marching crowd: more than 2,000 strong, walking barefoot, feeding themselves with a little bread and sugar. The march lasted a week. Gandhi was soon arrested, and 50,000 Indians immediately came out on strike. General Smuts was forced to negotiate, and signed with Gandhi a series of agreements in the interests of Indian communities.

In February 1930, now sixty years old, Gandhi formed the plan for the salt march. It was a dramatic construction, a collective epic. He assembled around him a nucleus of reliable militants, *satyagrahis* he had trained personally, on whose self-discipline and self-sacrifice he could depend. Seventy-eight militants were gathered for the expedition, the youngest aged sixteen. On 11 March, after evening prayer, Gandhi addressed a crowd of thousands requiring all his followers, in the event that he was arrested himself, to pursue the civil disobedience movement without him, calmly and peacefully. He set off at half past six the following morning, his long walking staff (a thick iron-bound bamboo) in his hand, surrounded by followers dressed like him in hand-woven cotton cloths, not quite eighty of them. When they reached the sea forty-four days later, they numbered several thousand.

As the days passed a routine became established: rise at six in the morning for prayers, meditation and chanting. Then, after ablutions and a meal, the procession would set off. Villages along the route took on a festive air; the roads were watered and scattered with leaves and flower petals to comfort the walkers' feet. Each time Gandhi would stop, calmly start to speak and urge people to cease all cooperation with the Empire: to boycott imported goods, to resign from any appointment as an official representative of the Empire. Above all, not to respond to provocation: to accept in advance the blows that would rain down, and allow themselves to be arrested without resisting. It was an immense success. Foreign correspondents followed the march by the day and sent it echoing round the world. The viceroy of India was at a loss for an answer. Gandhi's daily routine was immutable: prayer in the morning, walking through the day, hand-spinning cotton in the evening, writing articles for his journal at night. On 5 April, after walking for more than a month and a half, he came at last to Dandi, on the sea, and spent the night praying with his disciples. In the morning, at half past eight, he walked to the ocean, bathed in it, returned to the beach and performed in front of the assembled thousands the forbidden gesture by stooping and picking up a piece of salt, while the woman poet Sarojini Naidu cried: 'Hail, Deliverer!'

In the conception and accomplishment of that huge march one can discern several spiritual dimensions, all linked to Gandhi's convictions.

For a start, the slowness of the march constitutes a rejection of speed: the Mahatma's mistrust of the machine, accelerated consumption, mindless productivism. In a tract (Hind Swaraj) dating from November 1909, written on the ship taking him from London to South Africa, Gandhi attacks modern civilization. As well as a defence of non-violence, the text appears to be a defence of tradition, an apologia for slowness. For Gandhi, the real opposition wasn't between East and West, but rather between a civilization of speed, machinery and the accumulation of forces and one of transmission, prayer and manual labour. Which doesn't imply, however, that the choice is between the inertia of tradition and the conquerors' dynamism, but rather between two energies: the energy of the immemorial and the energy of change. Gandhi's choice was not between conservative torpor and adventurous boldness, but between calm force and perpetual agitation, the quiet illumination and the blinding flash.

Gandhi liked to think of that tranquil energy as maternal, feminine. For centuries in traditional societies, slow walking was the preserve of women: they would trek to distant wells to draw water, or set off down the paths to find plants and herbs. Men favoured violent expenditures of strength, appropriate to hunting: sudden attacks, short but very fast chases. Walking with Gandhi nurtured the slow energies of endurance. With walking, you are far removed from the lightning action, the fine deed, the exploit. It is done with that humility Gandhi loved: constant reminder of our gravity, our weakness. Walking is the condition of the poor. Humility, however, is not quite the same as poverty. It is the quiet recognition of our finiteness: we don't know everything, we can't do everything. What we know is nothing compared to the Truth, what we can do is nothing compared to Strength. And that recognition puts us in our proper place, locates us. In walking, far from any vehicle or machine, from any mediation, I am replaying the earthly human condition, embodying once again man's inborn, essential destitution. That is why humility is not humiliating: it just makes vain pretensions fall away, and thus nudges us towards authenticity. And there remains something proud in walking: we are upright. Humility in Gandhi's sense expressed our human dignity.

Walking also fitted with the theme of simplification he pursued all his life, taking the paths of non-possession (*aparigraha*). All the way from well turned-out young gent to the 'half-naked fakir' mocked by Churchill, Gandhi pursued his quest for stripping back in every area of life: clothing, housing, food and transport. From his early days in London wearing a greatcoat, double-breasted waistcoat and striped trousers, carrying a silver-knobbed walking stick, he gradually simplified his attire until in his last years he was dressed only in a loincloth of hand-woven white cotton. In South Africa, he left his comfortable rooms in Johannesburg to live on community farms, doing his full share of domestic chores. He made it a point of honour to travel only in third class, and by the end of his life ate nothing but fresh fruit and nuts. This simplification of life enabled him to go faster, straighter, more dependably to the essential. Walking is of a perfect simplicity: one foot in front of the other, there's no other way of advancing on two legs. But beyond that, the simplicity had a political aim. To live above your needs, Gandhi warned, is to be already exploiting your neighbour.

The task was to get rid of everything that might pointlessly encumber, embarrass, obstruct. Walking – marching – promoted an ideal of autonomy. Gandhi always set great value on indigenous crafts, produced locally. He gave the spinning-wheel a new lease of life, making it a duty to weave by hand every day. To work with your hands is to reject exploitation of others. The concept of marching fulfilled by itself the double ideal contained in the term *swadeshi*, employed by Gandhi to call on Indians to boycott British textiles, alcohol and manufactured goods. It signifies both 'proximity' and 'autarchy'. During a march, you make contact with people living their daily lives: you pass the fields where they work, and in front of their houses. You stop and talk. Walking is the right speed to understand, to feel close. Apart from that, you depend on yourself alone to advance. Given that you are up to it, your will alone is in charge, and you await only your own injunction. Neither machine nor fuel. Especially as walking can seem positively nutritious. Gandhi experienced that in the long 1930 march, when he arrived, after more than 390 kilometres on foot, looking more radiant than he had when he started.

Finally, Gandhi promoted through the marching movement a dimension of firmness and endurance: to keep going. That is essential, because walking calls for gentle but continuous effort. To suggest the sort of campaigns he hoped to wage, Gandhi at a political meeting in South Africa had invented a new word to describe his style of action: *satyagraha*. *Satyagraha* is the idea of force and truth rolled into one, the idea that one should be anchored firmly to truth as to a solid rock. Walking calls for determination, tenacity and willpower. Accordingly, during his years of struggle among the community structures he had set up here and there, Gandhi had managed to train some disciples along these lines. The key virtue of the *satyagrahi* is internal self-discipline. It means being ready to take blows without returning them, go quietly when unjustly arrested, and suffer humiliation, slander and insult without replying.

The mastery needed is double-sided: an ability to repress outbursts of rage and indignation, but also to weather moments of discouragement or cowardice; to remain calm, immobile, serene, sure of yourself and of the truth. Walking drains anger away, it purifies. When the *satyagrahis* reached the sea their indignation had been purged of hatred and anger: all that remained was a calm determination to break the law, because the law was unjust and iniquitous, making it a duty to transgress it, with the firmness and calm of prayer.

That perfect self-mastery is the precondition for a perfect love of all beings and for non-violence: *ahimsa*. This lies at the heart of the doctrine. Gandhi's non-violence wasn't a passive withdrawal, neutral resignation or submission. It gathered in a single sheaf, displayed in a single posture, all the dimensions identified above: dignity, discipline, firmness, humility, energy. Non-violence wasn't a simple rejection of force. It was more a matter of opposing physical force with the force of the soul alone. Gandhi did not say: make no resistance when the blows rain down, when the brutality redoubles. He said almost the opposite: resist with your entire soul by standing up for as long as possible, never surrendering any of your dignity, and without showing the slightest aggression or doing anything at all that might restore, between the whipper and the whipped, any reciprocity or equivalence in a community of violence and hate. On the contrary, show immense compassion for the one who is beating you. The relation should remain asymmetric in every respect: on one side a blind, physical, hate-filled rage, on the other a spiritual force of love. If you hold firm, then the relation is reversed; physical force degrades the one who uses it, who becomes a furious beast, while all human qualities are reflected in his prone victim, raised to a state of pure humanity by the attempt to lay him low. Non-violence puts violence to shame. To continue beating someone who opposes physical brutality with pure humanity, simple dignity, is to lose your honour and your soul there and then.

So it was with the next, terrible march, on which the *satyagrahis* set off in May 1930 to take possession of the Dharasana salt works in the name of the people. Gandhi had taken care to inform the viceroy in a letter of the march and its purpose, adding that the abrogation of the salt tax would be enough to cause its cancellation. But he was arrested, and unable to take part in the projected peaceful occupation of the salt pans. Four hundred police officers, armed with steel-tipped clubs, waited in the marshes. The *satyagrahis* slowly advanced, refusing to disperse. On reaching the police line they were savagely attacked, beaten to the ground and replaced by the next rank, beaten down in its turn. The *satyagrahis* didn't even try to protect themselves with their arms, but took the blows on their heads and shoulders. The police were seized with fury and some marchers were beaten to death on the ground. An American journalist, Webb Miller of the United Press Agency, witnessed the carnage and described the silent, determined advance of the *satyagrahis* 'walking with firm tread, head high', before falling. A painful silence punctuated only by

the thud of batons on flesh, breaking bones and a few involuntary groans. Several hundred were injured.

But the political gains of the 1930 movement didn't
live up to expectations, or to the grandeur of the act. The
Gandhi–Irwin pact (February 1931) was limited to minor
concessions, and the London conference attended by
Gandhi that September produced no decisive progress.
When World War II broke out in 1939, India was still largely
a subject country. Independence only came in August 1947,
and at the cost of the partition of India and Pakistan – the
worst of solutions, for Gandhi, who had always hoped for
freedom in unity and brotherhood.

Gandhi never stopped walking all through his life. He
attributed his excellent health to the habit. He walked to
the very end. The final years of his life saw his dream both
fulfilled and destroyed: freedom with disintegration. When
Britain was seriously preparing to abandon its Indian possessions, in the late 1940s, the rivalries between religious
communities, hitherto exploited by the British to divide
and rule, became intensified and soon exploded in violence,
leading to unprecedented massacres between Hindus,
Muslims and Sikhs.

In the winter of 1946 Gandhi took up his pilgrim's staff
once more, to travel on foot through two regions ravaged
by hatred (Bengal and Bihar), to walk from village to village
in the hope that here and there, by talking to everyone and
praying for all, he could revive the principles of love and fraternal unity. Between 7 November 1946 and 2 March 1947
he passed through several dozen villages, always on foot.

He walked because he wanted to make it clear that destitution was peaceful. He rose every morning at four to read and write, spun his daily measure of cotton, led prayers open to all, reciting Hindu and Muslim texts to show their peaceful convergence, and walked onward. He set off each morning chanting Rabindranath Tagore's terrible lines:

> If they answer not to thy call walk alone,
> if they are afraid and cower mutely facing the wall,
> O thou unlucky one,
> open thy mind and speak out alone.
> If they turn away, and desert you when crossing the wilderness,
> O thou unlucky one,
> trample the thorns under thy tread,
> and along the blood-lined track travel alone.

In September 1947 Gandhi performed 'the miracle of Calcutta': his simple presence, and announcement of a fast, were enough to extinguish the explosion of hatred that was ravaging the city. Independence had been proclaimed in August, and the announcement of Partition had provoked an unprecedented surge in inter-communal violence.

Gandhi died at the hands of a fanatical Hindu assassin on 30 January 1948.

The enduring image is that of an old man of nearly seventy-seven, walking all day leaning on the shoulder of his young niece, holding his pilgrim's staff in the other hand, going on foot from village to village, from massacre to massacre, supported by his faith alone, dressed like the poorest of the poor, underlining everywhere the reality of love and the absurdity of hatreds, and opposing the world's violence with the infinite peace of a slow, humble, unending walk.

The same image was retained by his indefatigable companion Nehru, the first leader of independent India. When he thought of Gandhi, what he most remembered was the salt march. As he wrote, back in 1930:

> Staff in hand, he goes along the dusty roads of Gujarat, clear-eyed and firm of step, with his faithful band trudging along behind him. Many a journey had he undertaken in the past, many a weary road had he traversed. But longer than any that have gone before is this last journey of his ... the goal is the independence of India and the ending of the exploitation of her millions.

25

Repetition

Walking is dull, repetitive and monotonous. That is all too true. But for that reason it is never tiresome. We mentioned earlier the need to distinguish between monotony and boredom. Boredom is an absence of plans, of prospects. You circle around yourself, at a loose end. Waiting, but not for *anything specific*: not expecting anything, but indefinitely suspended in empty time. The bored body reclines, gets up restlessly, jerks its arms about, steps out in one direction, then another, stops suddenly, starts again, fidgets. It is trying desperately to fill each second. Boredom is an empty rebellion against immobility; nothing to do, not even looking for something to do. You despair of yourself when bored. You tire of everything straight away, because it is on your own initiative. That faces you with the immense, unbearable ordeal of recognizing the poverty of your desires. Boredom is dissatisfaction repeated every second, disgust with beginnings: everything is wearisome from the start, because it's you who starts it.

Walking isn't tiresome in that way. It's simply monotonous. When you walk you are going somewhere, in motion, with a uniform tread. There is far too much regularity and rhythmic movement in walking to cause boredom, which is fed by vacuous agitation (mind rotating aimlessly in a stationary body). That is what led monks to suggest walking as a remedy for *acedia*, that insidious illness that gnaws at the soul. So it is generally right to contrast walking, which presupposes a purpose, with melancholic wandering.

Montaigne talked about his *'proumenoir'*. To stimulate his thinking, to move reflection forward, to deepen inventiveness, the mind needs the help of an active body: 'My thoughts sleep if I sit still; my fancy does not go so well by itself as when my legs move it.'

So there's no point in sitting over your desk when reflection is blocked. You need to get up and take a stroll. Walk, to get yourself moving, so that in sympathy with the body's surge the mind too will start moving again.

The mechanism here is one of pure release: walking as activation. Beyond that, through its regularity, walking provides an oscillation which this time can help poetry in verse: you get into the rhythm, establish yourself in the scansion. The English romantic Wordsworth is an example. When his

sister was asked where the poet worked, she waved vaguely
at the garden and said 'That's his office.' And in fact he did
compose his long lyrical poems while walking. He walked
up and down, murmuring, and used rhythmic body movements to help find the right lines.

Wordsworth is an unavoidable personage in any history
of walking, many experts considering him the authentic
originator of the long expedition. He was the first – at a
time (the late eighteenth century) when walking was the lot
of the poor, vagabonds and highwaymen, not to mention
travelling showmen and pedlars – to conceive of the walk
as a poetic act, a communion with Nature, fulfilment of the
body, contemplation of the landscape.

Christopher Morley wrote of him that he was 'one of the
first to use his legs in the service of philosophy'. Accordingly,
he discovered France on foot, walked over the Alps and
explored the English Lake District, using all his excursions
as material for his poems. His immense *Prelude*, a revealing
autobiographical poem worked on for most of his life and
published after his death, even resembles a superimposi-
tion of three walks: from childhood to maturity, along the
roads of France and Italy, and lastly that of balanced and
sonorous lines:

> Thus did I steal along that silent road
> My body from the stillness drinking in
> A restoration like the calm of sleep
> But sweeter far. Above, before, behind,
> Around me, all was peace and solitude.

The incomprehension and indeed hostility which Wordsworth encountered at the time underlines the real difference that exists between serious walking and the afternoon promenade. The promenade, in the big gardens of country houses, had been constructed as a social distinction. In those gardens with their complex walks, collusive shrubberies and providential intersections, people hid from and met one another. Hardly walking at all, really, but intermittent comings and goings, incessant dallying, shot through with witty conversation, flirtation and badinage, whispered confidences. The promenade was an occasion for deploying the art of seduction. It was in almost exact counterpoint to the day-labourer's trudge to the fields to sell his labour, or the homeless vagabond's endless quest for better luck along meandering paths. People didn't really walk along those garden paths: they danced.

But Wordsworth took to the road like a poor man, for pleasure and not through necessity. To general astonishment, he claimed to derive 'riches' from the experience. Over and above these enormous cultural innovations (the long expedition, the beauty of landscape), his poetry is infused with a walking rhythm, steady, monotonous, unshowy. It soothes without wearying, like the murmur of waves on a beach.

One other poet, also a walker, was able much later to recapture that remarkable monotony. Charles Péguy, most notably in his *Présentation de la Beauce*, made the pilgrimage to Notre-Dame de Chartres in 1912 to pray for the recovery

from typhoid of his son Pierre, composing interminable
verses on the road:

> We go straight forward, hands down in pockets,
> Without any kit, without clobber or talk,
> With a pace always even, no haste or refuge,
> From these fields right here to the next nearest there,
> You see us marching, the poor bloody infantry,
> We never take more than one step at a time.

Any very long walk can bring this sort of lyrical, mono-
chord psalmody to the lips. The Psalms themselves are
essentially pilgrim and walker chants: they either sing of
the sadness of exile, of the eternal stranger ('If I forget thee,
O Jerusalem ...'), or speak longingly of the Promised Land ('I
will lift up mine eyes unto the hills, from whence cometh
my help.').

Psalms do not call for much intellectual effort on the
level of meaning or content. They are meant to be uttered,
articulated, chanted, *embodied*. They should be actualized
in the body, and when chanted by several people, made
real in the body of a community. In India, those who go to
Pandharpur on foot still sing today the Psalms of Tukaram,
the illiterate Maratha small shopkeeper, born in 1698 into
the Shudra caste, the lowest one ('I am of the vile caste called
Tuka, I have read no books'), who met his god in the hills
and soon began to compose and recite verses, copied for
posterity by the literate disciples around him. Ever since,
Hindu pilgrims have chanted on the road the psalms of that
poet who couldn't read:

> Lord, that I might be
> Small pebble, big stone or dust
> On the Pandharpur road,
> To be trampled by the feet of saints!

Walking causes a repetitive, spontaneous poetry to rise naturally to the lips, words as simple as the sound of footsteps on the road. There also seems to be an echo of walking in the practice of two choruses singing a psalm in alternate verses, each on a single note, a practice that makes it possible to chant and listen by turns. Its main effect is one of repetition and alternation that St Ambrose compared to the sound of the sea: when a gentle surf is breaking quietly on the shore the regularity of the sound doesn't break the silence, but structures it and *renders it audible*. Psalmody in the same way, in the to-and-fro of alternating responses, produces (Ambrose said) a happy tranquillity in the soul. The echoing chants, the ebb and flow of waves recall the alternating movement of walking legs: not to shatter but to *make the world's presence palpable and keep time with it*. And just as Claudel said that sound renders silence accessible and useful, it ought to be said that walking renders *presence accessible and useful*.

So walking contains this huge power of repetition, repetition of the Same. It gives birth to psalms, which are the scanned realization of faith in the body's movement. That power of repetition can be found elsewhere, in a certain form of prayer. I am thinking especially here of what Orthodox spirituality calls in the *Philokalia* the 'prayer of the heart'. It consists of the simple repetition of an absolutely basic prayer, just a few words: 'Lord Jesus Christ, Son of God, have mercy on me, a poor sinner.' Simply repeating this prayer, counting it out minute by minute and hour by hour, turns each day into a continuous orison. The exercise in repetition may be accentuated by controlled breathing, making the first part of the mentally recited sentence ('Lord Jesus Christ, Son of God') correspond to the intake of breath, and the second part ('have mercy on me, a poor sinner') to its exhalation.*

The aim of this exercise in repetition is to achieve a state of concentration (by just doing one thing, repeating a single sentence), but not an intellectual concentration. Not a tightening of the mind, but a participation (with the whole body breathing and murmuring, all the senses attuned, all the soul's faculties reflecting the holy content of the prayer) of one's entire being in the recitation of the prayer. It's what the Orthodox Fathers called 'bringing the mind into the heart'. The great dangers as they saw it were of dispersion, distraction, dissipation, tantamount in their eyes to forgetting God. This neglect could also manifest itself in hard labour, which deadened the body, play, which stimulated the imagination, and meditation, which could become gratuitous speculation. The short, humble prayer from the heart, repetitive, absolutely obsessive, short-circuited all those alienations to lead us back, the Fathers said, to our inner Kingdom. The heart was the point of unification because it was the opening and energy of presence, liable

---

* This breathing also has a metaphysical meaning, inhalation signifying unification of the faculties and exhalation a necessary remission.

to deflect the temptations of the flesh as well as the drifts of the mind. Through repetition of this single sentence, which only has one meaning, the soul is entirely cleared of the false riches of thought and is absorbed in mental repetition of a single content.

Concentration, oneness, clearing out. Just a small phrase to repeat tirelessly: 'Lord Jesus Christ, have mercy on me, a poor sinner.' After a few minutes, a few hours, it is no longer a praying man but a man become prayer. He has become a continuous invocation of Christ, and little by little the terrible discomfort, the saturation of a mind suffocated by repeating the same thing, the mouth twisted by the mumbling of the lips, are succeeded in an instant, with sacral suddenness, by pure tranquillity (the famous *hêsukhia*, the Greek for 'peace'). The repetition becomes spontaneous, fluid, effortless, comparable to the heartbeat. And the monk finds total security in an indefinite unending murmur, in the ceaseless breathing of his prayer. Just as when you walk, there comes a moment when, from the monotonous repetition of the tread, there suddenly arises an absolute calm. You are no longer thinking of anything, no care can affect you, nothing exists but the regularity of the movement within you, or rather: the whole of you is the calm repetition of your steps.

Among the Fathers who taught it, that prayer from the heart was widely uttered from a submissive seated posture, chin on chest (an example being the Pseudo-Symeon or St Gregory of Sinai), immersed for long hours in repetition of the same sentence. But it was popularized in the West by the famous narrative of an anonymous nineteenth-century Russian pilgrim, who practised it while walking. It is the story of a simple soul who wanted fully to obey St Paul's exhortation to 'pray unceasingly'. A monk helped him to discover the *Philokalia* and the 'Jesus prayer': the determined fellow shut himself away in a garden for several weeks and repeated the prayer thousands of times, 6,000 a day, then 12,000. After many days of fatigue and effort, lassitude and boredom, the endless invocation of Christ's name came to inhabit his whole being, and became a source of inexhaustible joy and consolation. And when it had become almost as natural to him as breathing, he took to the road and walked tirelessly all day. He walked as he recited his prayer, to his own rhythm, without cease.

> This is how I go now, saying without pause the prayer to Jesus, dearer and sweeter to me than all else in the world. Sometimes, I cover more than seventy versts in a day and do not feel that I am moving; I only feel I am saying the prayer. When a violent chill takes hold of me, I recite the prayer with more attention and soon I am warmed through. When hunger becomes too sharp, I invoke the name of Jesus Christ more often and no longer recall feeling hungry. If I feel ill or that my back or legs are aching, I concentrate on the prayer and feel the pain no longer ... I have become rather odd. I have no worries about anything, nothing bothers me, nothing from outside interests me, I would rather be in permanent solitude; through habit, I have only a single need: to recite the prayer without cease.

That same insistence on regular repetition as a key to walking without fatigue is to be found in Tibetan spirituality, with the almost magical figure of the *lung-gom-pa*. *Lung-gom* consists of breathing and gymnastic exercises prolonged over several years, resulting in greatly increased agility and light-footedness. At the same time that he is training himself to control his breathing perfectly, the monk is learning how to tune the repetition of the mystical formulae to it with equal precision. Later, he will be able to harmonize them with the rhythm of his pace. At the end of his initiation, he becomes a *lung-gom-pa*. The monk is then capable, under certain circumstances, of walking very fast over enormous distances without fatigue. No doubt the necessary conditions include flat terrain, a desert landscape, nightfall or a starry night sky. In those ghostly spaces there is nothing to distract attention, concentration is at its maximum. The walker gathers himself, thinks of nothing, looks neither right nor left, focuses on a point ahead of him, starts walking, pronounces his cadenced formulae, and soon enters a hallucinatory trance state produced by the repetition of his tread, of the endlessly reproduced phrases, his steady breathing. And he covers great spans as if bounding over the ground.

Alexandra David-Neel recounts that during one of her long Himalayan walks, as she travelled across an immense isolated plateau, she saw a black dot in the distance which grew rapidly. She soon made out that it was a man coming towards her at very high speed. Her travelling companions told her the man was a *lung-gom-pa*, and that it was important not to speak to him or interrupt his progress, because he was in a state of ecstasy and might die if awakened. They watched him pass, his face expressionless, with open eyes, not running but rising with every step, like a light flimsy fabric tossed along by the wind.

Further Reading

GENERAL BIOGRAPHY

Joseph Amata, *On Foot: A History of Walking*, NYU Press, 2004.
Geoff Nicholson, *The Lost Art of Walking; The History, Science and Literature of Pedestrianism*, Riverhead Trade, 2009.
Rebecca Solnit, *Wanderlust: A History of Walking*, Penguin Books, 2001.
Henry David Thoreau, *Walking*, Watchmaker Publishing, 2010.

2. FREEDOMS

Jack Kerouac, *The Dharma Bums*, Penguin Modern Classics, 2000.
Swami Ramdas, *In Quest of God: The Saga of an Extraordinary Pilgrimage*, Blue Dove Press, 1994.

Gary Snyder, *The Practice of the Wild*, Counterpoint, 2010.

Heinrich Zimmer, *Philosophies of India*, Princeton University Press, 1969.

3. WHY I AM SUCH A GOOD WALKER – NIETZSCHE

R. J. Hollingdale, *Nietzsche: The Man and his Philosophy*, Cambridge University Press, 2001.

Friedrich Nietzsche, *Ecce Homo*, tr. Duncan Large, Oxford World's Classics, 2009.

Friedrich Nietzsche, 'The Wanderer and His Shadow', Part II of *Human, All Too Human*, tr. R. J. Hollingdale, Cambridge University Press, 1996.

Friedrich Nietzsche, *The Gay Science*, tr. Walter Kaufmann, Vintage, 1974.

Friedrich Nietzsche, *The Case of Wagner* & *The Birth of Tragedy*, tr. Walter Kaufmann, Random House, 2010.

Friedrich Nietzsche, *Thus Spake Zarathustra*, tr. Thomas Common, Dover Books, 2000.

Friedrich Nietzsche, *Selected Letters*, tr. Christopher Middleton, Hackett Publishing Co, 1996.

Rüdiger Safranski, *Nietzsche: A Philosophical Biography*, tr. Shelley Frisch, W. W. Norton, 2003.

6. THE PASSION FOR ESCAPE – RIMBAUD

Alain Borer, *Rimbaud in Abyssinia*, tr. Rosmarie Waldrop, William Morrow & Co., 1991.

Arthur Rimbaud, *Complete Works*, tr. Paul Schmidt, Harper Perennial Modern Classics, 2008.

Arthur Rimbaud, I Promise to Be Good: The Letters of Arthur Rimbaud, tr. Wyatt Mason, Modern Library, 2004.

Graham Robb, Rimbaud, Pan Macmillan, 2001.

7. SOLITUDES

Henry David Thoreau, Walden (Or Life in the Woods), Wilder Publications, 2008.

8. SILENCES

The Journal of Henry David Thoreau, 1837–1861, NYRB Classics, 2009.

Robert Louis Stevenson, Travels with a Donkey in the Cévennes & The Amateur Emigrant, Penguin Classics, 2004.

9. THE WALKER'S WAKING DREAMS – ROUSSEAU

Maurice Cranston, The Noble Savage: Jean-Jacques Rousseau in Exile and Adversity, University of Chicago Press, 1997.

Maurice Cranston, The Solitary Self: Jean-Jacques Rousseau, 1754–1762, University of Chicago Press, 1991.

Leo Damrosch, Jean-Jacques Rousseau: Restless Genius, Houghton Mifflin Harcourt, 2005.

Jean-Jacques Rousseau, Mon Portrait, Jules Ravenel, 1834; thelinguist. com.

Jean-Jacques Rousseau, Confessions, tr. Angela Scholar, Oxford World's Classics, 2000.

Jean-Jacques Rousseau, Discourse on the Origin of Inequality, tr. Anon, Dover, 2004.

Jean-Jacques Rousseau, *Reveries of the Solitary Walker*, tr. Russell Goulbourne, Oxford World's Classics, 2011.

10. ETERNITIES

Ralph Waldo Emerson, *Nature*, Penguin Books, 2008.

11. CONQUEST OF THE WILDERNESS – THOREAU

Henry David Thoreau, *Life Without Principle*, Forgotten Books, 2008.
Henry David Thoreau, *On the Duty of Civil Disobedience*, Wilder Publications, 2008.
Henry David Thoreau, *Slavery in Massachusetts*, Forgotten Books, 2008.
Henry David Thoreau, *Walden (Or Life in the Woods)*, Wilder Publications, 2008.
The Journal of Henry David Thoreau, 1837–1861, NYRB Classics, 2009.
Henry David Thoreau, *Walking*, Watchmaker Publishing, 2010.

12. ENERGY

Luther Standing Bear, *Land of the Spotted Eagle* (1933), University of Nebraska Press, 2006.
T. C. McLuhan, *Touch the Earth: A Self Portrait of Indian Existence*, Promontory Press, 1971.
Sylvain Tesson, *The Consolations of the Forest: Alone in a Cabin on the Siberian Taiga*, tr. Linda Coverdale, Rizzoli Ex Libris, 2013.
Henry David Thoreau, *A Winter Walk*, Theophania Publishing, 2012.

14. Regeneration and Presence

Lama Anagarika Govinda, *The Way of the White Clouds*, Rider, 2006.

15. The Cynic's Approach

R. Bracht Branham and Marie-Odile Goulet-Cazé, *The Cynic Movement in Antiquity and Its Legacy*, University of California Press, 2000.

The Cynic Philosophers: From Diogenes to Julian, tr. Robert Dobbin, Penguin Classics, 2013.

Diogenes the Cynic, *Sayings and Anecdotes with Other Popular Moralists*, tr. Robin Hard, 2012.

Epictetus, *Discourses and Selected Writings*, tr. Robert Dobbin, Penguin Classics, 2008.

Michel Foucault, *The Courage of Truth (Lectures at the College de France)*, Palgrave Macmillan, 2011.

Diogenes Laertius, *Lives of Eminent Philosophers*, Volumes I–II, tr. R. D. Hicks, Loeb Classical Library, 1925.

Plato, *Phaedrus*, tr. Christopher Rowe, Penguin Classics, 2005.

Xenophon, *Memorabilia*, tr. Amy C. Bonnette, Cornell University Press, 2001.

17. Melancholy Wandering – Nerval

Gérard de Nerval, *Selected Writings*, tr. Richard Sieburth, Penguin Classics, 1999.

Solomon Alhadef Rhodes, *Gérard de Nerval, 1808-1855: Poet, Traveler, Dreamer*, Philosophical Library, 1951.

18. A Daily Outing

Thomas De Quincey, *Last Days of Immanuel Kant and Other Writings*, Ulan Press, 2012.

Manfred Kuehn, *Kant: A Biography*, Cambridge University Press, 2002.

Rodolphe Töepffer, *Voyages en zigzag*, Hoëbeke, 1996.

Michel Vieuchange, *Smara: carnets de route*, Payot, 1996.

19. Strolls

Marcel Proust, *In Search of Lost Time*, tr. C. K. Scott Moncrieff and T. Kilmartin, 6 vols, Modern Library Classics, 2003.

Karl Gottlob Schelle, *L'Art de se promener*, tr. Pierre Deshusses, Payot & Rivages, 1996.

20. Public Gardens

Pierre Corneille, *The Liar*, tr. David Ives, Shakespeare Theatre Company ReDiscovery Series, Smith and Kraus, 2010.

Evaristo Gherardi, *Arlequin aux Tuileries & Les Promenades de Paris*, in *Le Théâtre italien de Gherardi*, J. B. Cusson and P. White, 1700.

For more on Gherardi and the Tuileries, see Michael Conan, *Performance and Appropriation: Profane Rituals in Gardens and Landscapes*, Dumbarton Oaks, 2007.

Charles Sorel, *Polyandre: Histoire comique* (1648), Klincksieck, 2010.

The Characters of Jean de La Bruyère, tr. Henri Van Laun, Scribner & Welford, 1885; bartleby.com.

21. THE URBAN FLÂNEUR

Louis Aragon, *Paris Peasant*, tr. Simon Watson-Taylor, Exact Exchange, 1999.

Charles Baudelaire, *Complete Poems*, tr. Walter Martin, Carcanet, 2007.

Charles Baudelaire, *Paris Spleen: Little Poems in Prose*, tr. Keith Waldrop, Wesleyan University Press, 2010.

Walter Benjamin, *The Writer of Modern Life: Essays on Charles Baudelaire*, various translators, Harvard University Press, 2006.

Walter Benjamin, *Charles Baudelaire: A Lyric Poet in the Era of High Capitalism*, Verso Books, 1977.

André Breton, *Nadja*, tr. Richard Howard, Penguin Twentieth Century Classics, 1999.

Guy Debord, *The Society of the Spectacle*, tr. D. Nicholson-Smith, Zone Books, 1994.

Thierry Paquot, *Art of the Siesta: A Book About Stealing Moments of Repose*, tr. Ken Hollings, Universe, 2005.

22. GRAVITY

Michael F. Cleary, *The Essential Tao: An Initiation into Taoism through the Authentic Tao Te Ching and the Inner Teachings of Chuang-Tzu*, Harper San Francisco, 1991.

See also complete translation of the *Zhuangzi* by Nina Correa, at daoisopen.com.

24. MYSTIC AND POLITICIAN – GANDHI

Louis Fischer, *Gandhi: His Life and Message for the World*, Signet Classics, 2010.

Mohandas K. Gandhi, *Non-Violent Resistance (Satyagraha)*, Dover Publications, 2001.

Mohandas K. Gandhi, *Hind Swaraj or Indian Home Rule*, Navajivan Publishing, 2008.

Mohandas K. Gandhi, *Autobiography: The Story of My Experiments with Truth*, CreateSpace Independent Publishing Platform, 2012.

Betsy Kuhn, *The Force Born of Truth*, Twenty-First Century Books, 2011.

Webb Miller, *I Found No Peace: The Journal of a Foreign Correspondent*, Literary Guild, 1936.

Jawaharlal Nehru, *Toward Freedom: The Autobiography of Jawaharlal Nehru*, The John Day Company, 1942.

25. REPETITION

Alexandra David-Neel, *Magic and Mystery in Tibet*, Souvenir Press, 2007.

Psalms of Maratha Saints: One Hundred and Eight Hymns Translated from the Marathi by Nicol Macnicol [1920], Cornell University Library, 2009.

Michel de Montaigne, *Essays*, tr. John. M. Cohen, Penguin Books, 1993.

Charles Péguy, *Présentation de la Beauce à Notre-Dame de Chartres*, Gallimard, 1946.

The Philokalia, tr. K. Ware and P. Sherrard, 4 vols, Faber and Faber, 1979, 1982, 1986, 1999.

The Way of a Pilgrim & A Pilgrim Continues His Way, tr. Olga Savin, Shambhala, 2001.

William Wordsworth, *The Major Works: Including The Prelude*, Oxford World's Classics, 2008.

On the Typeface

This book is set in Trinité, designed by the Dutch book designer Bram de Does in 1978–82 for the Enschedé printing company in Haarlem.

Trinité possesses perhaps the strongest calligraphic flavour in a contemporary book face, with its lilting stems, pronounced accents, and the extravagant hook of the f. Its curved structures maintain a humanist form despite the thin even strokes, unbracketed serifs and subtle cant.

The typeface family consists of a narrow and a wide version, both of which have three different grades of ascender and descender heights – hence the name Trinité.

According to de Does, the success of Trinité steered him away from his original plan to become an organic farmer.